IMPERIALISM

AND COLONIALISM

GEORGE H. NADEL

Honorary Nuffield Fellow
The Warburg Institute, University of London

and

PERRY CURTIS

THE MACMILLAN COMPANY, NEW YORK

COLLIER-MACMILLIAN LIMITED, LONDON

First Printing

Library of Congress catalog card number: 64–16856

The Macmillan Company, New York
Collier-Macmillan Canada, Ltd., Toronto, Ontario

Printed in the United States of America

CONTENTS

26994

MAIN THEMES IN EUROPEAN HISTORY

Bruce Mazlish, General Editor

THE ROLE OF RELIGION IN MODERN
EUROPEAN HISTORY
edited by Sidney A. Burrell

THE DEVELOPMENT OF WESTERN TECHNOLOGY
SINCE 1500
edited by Thomas Parke Hughes

THE DEVELOPMENT OF THE MODERN STATE
edited by Heinz Lubasz

THE RISE OF SCIENCE IN RELATION TO SOCIETY
edited by Leonard M. Marsak

POPULATION MOVEMENTS IN MODERN
EUROPEAN HISTORY
edited by Herbert Moller

IMPERIALISM AND COLONIALISM
edited by George H. Nadel and Perry Curtis

Other volumes in preparation

FOREWORD

History, we are frequently told, is a seamless web. However, by isolating and studying the strands that compose the tapestry of man's past, we are able to discern the pattern, or patterns, of which it is comprised. Such an effort does not preclude a grasp of the warp and woof, and the interplay of the strands; rather, it eventually demands and facilitates such a comprehension. It is with this in mind that the individual volumes of the MAIN THEMES series have been conceived.

The student will discover, for example, that the population changes discussed in one volume relate to the changes in technology traced in another volume; that both changes are affected by, and affect in turn, religious and intellectual developments; and that all of these changes and many more ramify into a complicated historical network through all the volumes. In following through this complex interrelationship of the parts, the student recreates for himself the unity of history.

Each volume achieves its purpose, and its appeal to a general audience, by presenting the best articles by experts in the field of history and allied disciplines. In a number of cases, the articles have been translated into English for the first time. The individual volume editor has linked these contributions into an integrated account of his theme, and supplied a selected bibliography by means of footnotes for the student who wishes to pursue the topic further. The introduction is an original treatment of the problems in the particular field. It provides continuity and background for the articles, points out gaps in the existing literature, offers new interpretations, and suggests further research.

The volumes in this series afford the student of history an unusual opportunity to explore subjects either not treated, or touched upon lightly in a survey text. Some examples are population—the dramatis personae of history; war—the way of waging peace by other means; the rise of technology and science in relation to society; the role of religious and cultural ideas and institutions; the continuous ebb and flow of exploration and colonialism; and the political and economic works contrived by modern man. Holding fast to these Ariadne threads, the student penetrates the fascinating labyrinth of history.

BRUCE MAZLISH
General Editor

INTRODUCTION

Imperialism and colonialism are words that attract and repel. Their ambiguity appeals to the propagandist who makes a virtue of imprecision and exasperates the serious student who searches in vain for some consensus about their meaning. For better or worse these terms have become part of our daily diet of political abstractions, and there are few signs that they will be abandoned for less controversial alternatives. Indeed, the word imperialism has acquired universality. It acknowledges no language barriers and means all things to all men. Associations of empire with the majestic imperium of Rome or with the glittering, if hollow, crown of the Hapsburgs have long since given way to images of white men ruthlessly exploiting native populations in Africa, Asia, and the New World, or of European bondholders manipulating the foreign policies of their governments in order to increase the returns on overseas investments.

By imperialism we mean the extension of sovereignty or control, whether direct or indirect, political or economic, by one government, nation or society over another together with the ideas justifying or opposing this process. Imperialism is essentially about power both as end and means. Behind the stirring slogans, the martial symbols, and the institutional façade of empire can be found superior military, economic, political, or moral power. Underlying all forms of imperialism is the belief—at times unshakable—of the imperial agent or nation in an inherent right, based on moral superiority as well as material might, to impose its pre-eminent values and techniques on the "inferior" indigenous nation or society.

Imperialism generally involves the collision of two or more cultures and a subsequent relationship of unequal exchange between or among them. What confuses the issue has been the inability of men to analyze their real motives for territorial or cultural expansion and to separate them from rationalizations devised after the fact.

According to expert opinion, the term imperialism made its official debut in England in the mid-nineteenth century to characterize the aggressive policies of Napoleon III.[1] Later, English radicals and liberals attached this label to the flamboyant actions of Disraeli, who, during his second term as prime minister (1874–1880), secured for Britain a controlling interest in the Suez Canal and added "Empress of India" to Queen Victoria's other titles. By the mid-1880's the term was no longer identified with merely a crude expansionist mood ("jingoism") or displays of brute force and gun-boat diplomacy. Connoting power, prestige, dignity, and affluence, "imperialism" was invoked by some even as a panacea to cure political, social, and economic ills at home. It took the troubles in South Africa, culminating in the Boer War (1899–1902), to remove the honor and the glory from this word—a word whose history is very much shorter than that of the phenomena which it describes.

The readings in this book deal with two phases of Western European expansion overseas. From these periods of prodigious activity on the part of Europeans emerged two clusters of colonial empires, which we have labeled the old and the new. For convenience the era of the American and French Revolutions has been chosen as the watershed separating the first and second empires. We have made no attempt to cover more than a fragment of this historic movement of men, ideas, and material wealth across the seas: the articles in this volume refer to only a few facets of the maritime or colonial empires created by European nations after the voyages of discovery. Our exclusive concern with overseas empires, moreover, does not mean that the great land empires of Caesar Augustus, the Carolingians, Hapsburgs, Romanovs, or Napoleon Bonaparte are not equally deserving of study. Limitations of space have further forced us to neglect the empires of the Netherlands, Belgium, and Italy and to single out one empire only, the British, for closer attention in our Introduction. For the same reason we have omitted discussion of Soviet expansion since 1945, which some observers consider equivalent to the traditional patterns of imperialism in Europe. But to list all the omissions of this anthology would amount to writing a definitive history of imperialism and colonialism. Our intention, rather, is to provide the reader with as many insights as possible into the modern European imperial process that has so profoundly affected the history of mankind.

Despite the danger of generalizing about a subject so rife with ex-

[1] R. Koebner, "The Concept of Economic Imperialism," *Economic History Review,* 2nd Series, II, No. 1 (1949), 1–29; and "The Emergence of the Concept of Imperialism," *Cambridge Journal,* V (1952) 726–41.

ceptions and paradoxes, it is possible to make at least two broad state-
ments about imperialism. First and most obvious, imperial expansion has
never been a uniquely European experience. Assyrians, Phoenicians,
Ottoman Turks, Huns, Tartars, the warrior nations of Africa and the
New World—to name but a few—have all created empires through
conquest and colonization. Since extension of power over others has
been one of the chief preoccupations of mankind throughout recorded
history, radical changes in imperialism have more frequently occurred
in its theory than in its universal practice. Second, the motives underlying imperialism are those of the countless men or nations that acquired
and ruled over colonial empires. Anyone who believes in the diversity
of human behavior and who rejects cosmic solutions or single causes in
history will not hesitate to point out the inconsistencies, mysteries, and
even absurdities of imperialism. In this sense the study of empires provides an effective point of departure for exploring the meaning of
history itself.

Whereas "imperialism" enjoyed at least a genuine if fleeting respect-
ability, "colonialism" has been weighed down with original sin almost
since its inception. To some, colonialism has meant imperialism as seen
from the colonial vantage point; and, indeed, that all colonialisms have
been implied by imperial expansion, but that not all imperial expansions
imply colonialism, is undeniable.[2] But "colonialism" is most commonly
used today to connote the oppression, humiliation, or exploitation of
indigenous peoples. This usage, although well justified, has its disadvantages. It withdraws attention from other facets of colonialism, which
are important to the student of European history. There is, for example,
the transplanting and modifying of European institutions overseas;
colonial policies and administrative practices, as they reflect the social
and political disposition of the mother country; and the opposition
within the mother country to owning colonies (rather than the opposition of colonies to being owned by the mother country). These topics
are taken up in the pages which follow and are included in some of
the readings. Colonialism as a term of justified reproach or unjustified
abuse, conveying simply domination of colored peoples by whites, is
not our concern. The same is true of its successor-word, neo-colonialism,
which denotes indirect domination, usually economic or cultural, of
countries formerly colonies but now politically independent.

[2] For a discussion of the relationship of these terms, see Hans Kohn, "Reflec-
tions on Colonialism," in Robert Strausz-Hupé and Henry W. Hazard (eds.),
The Idea of Colonialism (New York: 1958), pp. 2 ff.; and A. P. Thornton,
"Colonialism," *International Journal*, XVII (1962), 335–57.

Colonialism, as Herbert Lüthy argues succinctly in his article, "Colonization and the Making of Mankind," is an abusive term designed to stigmatize countries that have owned colonies at some stage in their development. Lüthy prefers the less polemical word colonization to describe the process of cultural transmission that has brought mankind to the present level of civilization. It is a dynamic, self-perpetuating process because the values, customs, and techniques of a society continue to take root in other soil long after the parent plant has withered or died. "The history of colonization," he contends, "is the history of humanity itself."

The Old Empires

I

The initial impetus for overseas exploration and conquest came from Mediterranean civilizations. For centuries the Mediterranean, and Rome in particular, had been the center of the Western world. But with the decline of the spiritual and temporal power of Latin Christendom, a new secular spirit, humanist in orientation, radiated from the Italian city states. During the fourteenth and fifteenth centuries forces were developing that would eventually remove the physical and psychological barriers to the discoveries of lands beyond the narrow horizon and shift the center of European gravity to the Atlantic seaboard, to the new monarchies of Spain, Portugal, France, and England. It was no accident that the age of discovery coincided with the emergence of centralizing and self-assertive nation states in Western Europe. To brave the unknown perils of the Atlantic, Western Europeans needed more than the intellectual and esthetic skills with which Italian humanism had provided them. The adventurers of the fifteenth century required ships capable of crossing oceans, navigational instruments, firearms, and, frequently, support from strong governments. The advantages of national unity, military prowess gained through generations of conflict with the Moors, and maritime experience made Portugal and Spain the natural springboards for the first voyages of discovery across the Atlantic and around the coast of Africa to the Indies.

Without a number of innovations in cartography, astronomical observation, and shipbuilding the search for a route to the Indies would never have succeeded. It was this revolution in navigational aids, in ship design (the square-rigged caravel), and in firearms—much of it achieved through contact with Arab civilization—that transformed a series of reconnaissance expeditions, financed by the bankers and merchants of Southern Europe as well as by the specie of the New World, into a full-scale colonial enterprise.

It is still a moot point whether the discovery of America was an accident and an unwelcome surprise to those who believed in a short cut to the Orient. Disappointment eventually turned to joy, however, once the successors of Columbus began to penetrate the interior of Mexico and South America. The period 1520 to 1550 has been called the age of the conquistador in honor of those hardened veterans of the crusades who followed in the wake of the explorers. For centuries the profession of arms and the pursuit of trade had gone together, and the conquistadores were no exception to the rule. Bearing cross and sword they set sail in caravels, they explored, and they conquered. Even more important many of them stayed. Out of such motives as curiosity, avarice, and religious zeal emerged the first European settlements in the New World.

One of the problems that now arose involved the rights and obligations of European conquerors or settlers. During the first half of the sixteenth century Spanish jurists, learned in canon and natural law, developed a theory of constitutional government. Although their conception of limited sovereignty gradually succumbed to absolutism at home, it had a profound influence across the Atlantic, where the duty to convert and educate the natives of the New World had been an integral part of the bulls of demarcation. Overseas expansion also raised a number of questions about the rights of conquest, the disposition of native lands, and the legal status of the Indians. Various schools of jurists and scholars sought to provide answers to these crucial questions. The result was a controversy remarkable for the fervor, erudition, and ingenuity with which it was conducted. If Spanish theories of empire failed to impress the Indians with the advantages of colonization, the attempt to found colonial policy on the rule of law had vital implications for the future.

Having undertaken their expeditions at considerable risk and cost to themselves, the conquistadores naturally resented interference from Spain. But the Crown had no intention of allowing these intrepid commanders to build their own empires in the New World. However, despite much persistence the House of Castile never achieved the goal of regulating every facet of life in the new colonies. In his article,

"Spanish Colonial Theory and Practice," Professor Woodrow Borah traces the development of quasi-representative institutions in Hispanic America. If the Crown was theoretically omnipotent, in practice the independent character of many Spanish settlers in the New World as well as the sale of colonial offices after 1559 served to impede the centralizing forces within the empire.

The Spanish Crown found some solace for this setback in the form of specie from Mexico, Hispaniola, and Peru. Since most of the gold and silver mines were privately owned, however, the Crown received about 20 percent of their production, and this sum amounted to only a fraction of its income from all sources. In the period 1503 to 1660 the total influx of treasure into Spain has been estimated at 447,820,932 pesos.[3] Naturally, the annual treasure fleets that conveyed these riches to Spain attracted the unwelcome attention of buccaneers, privateers, and corsairs from the other maritime nations of the world.

Among the first Europeans since classical times to found formal colonies overseas, the Portuguese were more businesslike and less legalistic than the Spanish in their colonial empire. Charles R. Boxer's study, "The Portuguese in Brazil," reveals the character and activities of the early settlers in this colony. Initially, Brazil was regarded as a way station to the Indies, and the absence of silver deposits comparable to those at Potosí did not enhance its value in the eyes of the Portuguese. Not until 1549 did the Crown assume official control of the administration, and only at the end of the century did Brazil become a prime producer of sugar. Before the European sugar market brought new wealth to the Portuguese colonists, Brazil's chief exports were hides, tobacco, some cotton, and the eponymous brazilwood, from which a valuable red dye was extracted. During the first half of the seventeenth century the large plantations in the northeast made Brazil the world's leading sugar producer. But this monopoly was soon broken up by French, Dutch, and English interlopers.

The Portuguese were also among the first Europeans to profit from the slave trade. With their merchant fleet and their footholds along the coast of Africa they were in an ideal position to exploit the human resources of the interior. The demand for Negro labor in the New World increased rapidly once the African's capacity for work in tropical conditions had proved superior to that of the Indian. During

[3] This figure includes both public and private imports but excludes smuggled specie. See Earl J. Hamilton, *American Treasure and the Price Revolution in Spain 1501-1650* (Cambridge, Mass.: 1934), pp. 32–42.

the seventeenth century some 5,000 Negroes crossed the Atlantic every month in the fetid holds of ships; and in the next century an estimated seven million slaves were transported to the New World. The ruthless search for cheap labor provides one of the main elements of continuity between the first and second empires. Without this indispensable tool many colonial ventures would have ended in abject failure. In this respect Africa's most precious raw material for more than three centuries was neither gold, copper, nor precious stones but manpower. The arrival of Negro slaves in Spanish, Portuguese, and other European colonies also added a new and ominous note to the problem of miscegenation.

II

During the century and a half following the discovery of gold and silver in the New World the influx of bullion into Europe produced a price revolution that materially affected the economic structure as well as the social and political stability of Europe. By 1650 prices were approximately three times what they had been in 1500, and those men dependent on fixed incomes suffered the consequences of steady inflation. In the same period Portugal and Spain struggled to preserve their overseas holdings against the encroachments of three aggressive powers to the north. The Dutch, English, and French not only created colonial empires at the expense of their Iberian neighbors but also quarrelled incessantly among themselves over the spoils. This intensification of the rivalry for colonies and trade reflected the changing political and economic scene in Europe. Throughout the turbulent seventeenth century the focus of power and wealth gradually moved north. The new balance of power was symbolized by the alliance after 1688 of England and Holland—two bitter rivals for commercial supremacy—against the expansionist France of Louis XIV. Unable to mobilize their national resources as effectively as France or England, both Portugal and Spain played secondary roles in Louis's bid for European hegemony. While the production of precious metals in the New World fell off sharply after 1630, the Dutch snatched the bulk of the slave trade from the Portuguese, only to lose it in turn to the English. The struggle among the great powers for paramountcy in Europe hopelessly embroiled the New World in the quarrels of the old. What decided the outcome of this contest was not just superior military or naval force but often the nature of colonial policy.

Mixed motives also characterized the colonizing activities of the

English, Dutch, and French. Less zealous than the Spanish in their desire to convert the heathen, the northern powers were nevertheless conscious of a Christianizing mission. Although the English came to the imperial scene relatively late, their advantageous position at the gateway to Europe as well as their approach to colonization helped to atone for this tardiness.

Just as the balance of power in Europe moved north, so too in the New World the main sphere of imperial activity shifted from Brazil, Peru, and Central America to the Caribbean islands and the coast of North America. Besides providing access to the Atlantic fisheries this coastal region supplied furs, timber and other ships' stores. The prospect of big profits from tobacco planting and the search for precious metals or the mythical northwest passage from the Atlantic to Asia also lured explorers and settlers to North America.

All these materialistic motives have been subsumed under the generic and controversial term mercantilism. The mercantile system transcended the goal of maintaining a favorable balance of trade. More than a monetary system, it was a way of life, a universal doctrine designed to create an all powerful nation state. In his summary account, **"Colonies and the Mercantile System,"** Hugh E. Egerton has examined the vital connection between economic theory and colonial empire. Colonies figured prominently in the grand designs of the mercantilist school. The strict control of traffic to and from the colonies, the creation of commercial companies like the East India Company, and the restrictions imposed on colonial manufactures were all responses to this form of political and economic warfare. Under mercantilist auspices the state took an active interest in overseas exploration and colonization. However crude and unrealistic in theory mercantilism influenced the policies of every major power to some degree.

III

Colonial theories and practices varied widely in the old empires. The Spanish excelled at political centralization and the Portuguese proved more adept in economic matters. If anything, the Spanish Crown was too fastidious about colonial rule. So much attention was paid to legal and political formalities in the empire that often minor decisions were referred to Madrid. The *audiencias* or courts of appeal possessing executive as well as judicial powers were dominated by Spanish lawyers who advised and served as checks on viceroys and governor-generals.

The Portuguese, on the other hand, encouraged decentralization in Brazil by conferring hereditary rights on the captains or *donatários* who ruled over vast estates like semi-feudal magnates. After the Portuguese-Spanish "marriage" in 1580 the two colonial systems drew closer together in theory if not in practice. In 1604 Portugal established a Council of the Indies similar to that in Spain, and four years later the first *audiencia* was held at Bahia in Brazil. To assure an adequate labor supply the Spanish Crown granted to individual settlers in America the right—known as the *encomienda*—to collect tributes from native towns and villages. Resembling at times a system of forced labor and military levies, the *encomienda* led to disputes in the colonies as well as among jurists in Spain and was later modified, if not purged of its abuses, in the *repartimento*.

Nowhere was variation more evident than in the English empire. Although they could not match the Dutch in financial acumen and in the size or efficiency of their merchant fleet, the English believed in founding settlement colonies and not just ports of call en route to the Indies. The first English settlers in America encountered far more difficulties with the Indians than had the Portuguese or Spanish. Because of the existence of Ireland, however, the English were not entirely innocent of the colonizing process. Men like Raleigh and his half-brother Sir Humphrey Gilbert had gained valuable experience in the technique of planting colonies on hostile soil through attempts to pacify the Irish. Owing to the reluctance of whole families and of skilled workers to emigrate to the remote American coast, the promoters of colonial enterprises had to devote much thought to publicity. During Queen Elizabeth's reign (1558–1603) a steady stream of pamphlets and circulars appeared advertising the riches that lay in store for adventurous Englishmen. One of the most notable of these publicists, Richard Hakluyt, insisted that the menace of Spain made the founding of colonies and naval bases a matter of national security. From their bases in North America English ships could sail north to fish the Newfoundland Banks or south to raid the Spanish treasure fleets.

Hakluyt and other advocates of empire not only stressed the value of colonies as producers of raw materials and consumers of finished goods but also reminded Englishmen of their duty to spread the Gospel among the savages of the New World. More pragmatic in colonial policies than either the Spanish or the French, the English preached the obligation of converting the heathen but in practice tended to regard the Indians with much the same contempt that Cromwell reserved for

the Irish. In Hispanic America, by contrast, far more was done to bring
the natives into the pale of European civilization.

Besides joint-stock or chartered companies the English developed
such expedients for colonization as the proprietary colony analogous
to the Portuguese captaincies in Brazil, and Crown colonies nominally
under direct royal control. What English colonies in America lacked
in natural resources and uniformity they made up for in the number
and industriousness of the colonists themselves. In the decade 1630–
40, for example, over 40,000 English and Scottish emigrants crossed
the ocean to settle in New England and the Caribbean. And by 1700
the thirteen colonies contained some 500,000 inhabitants.

The Europeans who emigrated to the New World came from
every stratum of society except the highest. There was no stereotype.
In a period when religious or political convictions as well as mis-
demeanors could lead to harsh penalties, many of the early settlers
were ostensibly criminals seeking freedom of conscience and economic
opportunity. Some of the most versatile emigrants to Brazil were
the crypto-Jews expelled from Spain; and the extent to which the
American colonies served as a haven for the victims of religious and
political persecution needs no further emphasis. Economic and social
forces played an important part in luring Europeans overseas. In
England younger sons of the gentry who inherited little more than a
name often turned to colonial ventures. Along with the educated,
the enterprising, the oppressed, the curious, and the idealistic went some
of the riffraff of Europe. Not all stayed. Many of the Spaniards
who made their fortunes in the New World returned to spend them
at home; and a number of American colonists went back to England
having failed to find the utopia of their dreams. Those who stayed
behind to endure the rigors of an inhospitable country were making
not just a new start but, more important, a new society.[4]

IV

The eighteenth century witnessed a series of violent oscillations in
the fortunes of colonial empires. England emerged from the pro-

[4] For further details of the old empires the reader is referred to J. H. Parry,
The Establishment of the European Hegemony 1415–1715 (New York: 1961)
and *The Age of Reconnaissance* (London: 1963). Herbert I. Priestley, *The Coming of the White Man, 1492–1848* (4th ed.; New York: 1961) deals with North
America. The classic work on mercantilism is Eli F. Heckscher, *Mercantilism*,
2 vols. (2nd ed.; New York: 1955).

tracted wars of the mid-century as a world power rivaled only by France in the size and affluence of her empire. Since the peace of Utrecht (1713), some English merchants had profited from the right to traffic in slaves across the Atlantic. The Spanish navy could not prevent the flow of English capital and illicit goods into Hispanic America. Although the Dutch clung tenaciously to their commercial and financial predominance, they could not compete against either France or England in population and natural resources. Rather than the luxury goods of India and Asia, it was the sugar crop of the West Indies that represented the most concentrated and coveted form of wealth. In the eighty-year period 1713–92, British possessions in the Caribbean exported £162,000,000 worth of sugar and other products to the mother country. The lucrative slave trade formed one leg of the triangular route from England to Africa to the West Indies and thence home. So valuable were the plantations of the Caribbean to Western European economies that England alone sacrificed thousands of soldiers, most of whom died from disease, while defending her interests in the West Indies.

In England lingering faith in mercantilist dogma, the jealousy of powerful commercial interests, and the intoxicating effects of the Seven Years' War forced colonial policies further away from a realistic appraisal of colonial aspirations. Insensitivity to the altered mood and situation in the American colonies characterized not only most members of the ruling classes in England but also civilian and military officials who were on the scene. The joint failure of Parliament and the Crown to appreciate the reciprocal process inherent in the colonization of North America ended in the War of Independence and the separation of political ties with the United Kingdom. The American Revolution had a traumatic effect on many Europeans as well as Englishmen. In his chapter, **"The Fall of the First British Empire,"** Professor Klaus E. Knorr analyzes the degree to which the loss of the thirteen colonies re-enforced or dispelled English illusions about empire. Although they were not the first to experience the sensation of militant colonial nationalism, Englishmen were chagrined to find American colonists invoking English constitutional precedents as justification for their revolt against the Crown. The paradox of an imperial government based on the consent of propertied interests denying this same principle to fellow-subjects across the sea was underlined by the War of Independence. Later those countries that ignored the lessons of the American Revolution by trying to maintain a double standard within their empires invariably found the cost of such a policy exorbitant.

The New Empires

I

Just as the first colonial empires emerged in an age when new forces were challenging traditional assumptions and institutions, so the new empires were created during a period of equally momentous change. Behind this second great outthrust of Europe lay revolutions in political and economic organization, in science, and in the attitudes of men about their place in the universal order. What was new about the new empires was not so much the amalgam of motives and methods involved but the metamorphosis of European nations and societies into far more complex and powerful units. Both empires shared one common feature: the fact of expansion itself.[5]

Since the colonial empires of the nineteenth century were established at different times and for different reasons any chronological division between the old and the new must be somewhat arbitrary. Despite many popular candidates for this claim, no single date marks the beginning of the so-called "new imperialism." In order to separate the two main phases of European overseas colonization we have chosen the years 1775 to 1815 as those of transition. This choice can be justified by the changes in the structure of European society and politics associated with these decades of revolution. The loss of the American colonies, moreover, seemed to bear out the physiocratic view of colonies as analogous to fruit that ripened and eventually fell from the parent tree. During the last half of the eighteenth century the

[5] The second or new empires have been examined individually and in detail, but there are few comparative studies of any merit. For too long the literature of imperialism has been dominated by the white man's point of view and has reflected the failure to make judicious use of the social sciences in analyzing the impact as well as the origins of imperial expansion. Strictures on the traditional treatment of imperialism may be found in L. J. Ragatz, "Must We Rewrite the History of Imperialism?" *Historical Studies, Australia and New Zealand*, 21 (1953), 90–98. See also his bibliography, *The Literature of European Imperialism, 1815–1939* (Washington: 1944). William L. Langer, *The Diplomacy of Imperialism, 1890–1902* (2nd ed.; New York: 1956) offers a useful introduction to the competition for empire among the great powers at the end of the nineteenth century and contains an annotated bibliography.

social, political, and intellectual ferment that spread through Hispanic America as well as British North America ushered in a new era in colonial relations. And in Europe the rise of industrialism, democratic ideas, and laissez-faire theories all served to expedite the death of the old colonial system.

Among the distinctive features of the new empires were a shift in emphasis, after mid-century, from private to national aspects of colonization, the relative abundance of capital for overseas investment, and the increasingly bitter agitation against imperialism itself. First, encroachments by the state into traditionally private spheres of activity affected the course of empire. No longer were colonies treated as the private property of the Crown (the Belgian Congo excepted). The decline of the old colonial system combined with extensions of the franchise to make imperial policy ever more subject to review by national legislatures or professional bureaucracies. By 1914 all colonial empires had to some extent become politicized. Second, the maturing capitalist economies of Western Europe, above all the industrial-financial complex in Great Britain, created neeeds that could apparently be satisfied only through investment in other parts of the world. Compared with the old, the new empires were notable for the outlay of capital that went into their development.

The new imperialism was also accompanied by a steady growth in the size and influence of the anti-imperialist cause. By 1900 imperialism had been indicted on many different counts and with a passion that made Adam Smith's denunciation of the mercantile system appear innocuous. To the radicals of the Manchester School, men like Cobden, Bright, and Goldwin Smith, colonial imperialism represented the extension overseas of the evils afflicting European societies. Imperialism, then, was an effective stalking horse for those whose real concern lay with social and economic injustices at home. The opponents of empire championed domestic reform or, in the case of Lenin, revolution. During the Boer War the radical Liberal, John A. Hobson, tried to shatter what was left of the illusion that British political genius or altruism had built the empire. In his provocative work, *Imperialism: A Study* (1902), Hobson declared that only a drastic reform of the capitalist system could remedy the rank inequities fostered by imperialism. This economic interpretation of the new imperialism is examined by David K. Fieldhouse in his article, **"The New Imperialism: The Hobson-Lenin Thesis Revised."** Even if the ghost of Hobson is not finally laid by this skillful analysis of imperial activity in the late nineteenth century, at least Fieldhouse has succeeded in disentangling the strands of fact and fiction that have so long confused the issue.[6]

The new empires also differed from the old in their location. In general they were carved out of the African continent, Asia, and the South Pacific. This reversion to Africa and the Far East was influenced by the needs of European industries for such tropical raw materials as oil and rubber and by myths about the vast, untapped markets of China. In Africa the vested interests of slave traders, the virulence of tropical diseases, the hostility of many tribes, and the difficulties of terrain and climate had long prevented white men from penetrating the interior. During the nineteenth century, however, the abolition of the slave trade as well as advances in medicine and firepower gradually opened up the hinterland to Europeans. The last two decades of the century witnessed the almost legendary scramble for Africa. Precipitated by King Leopold's enterprises in the Congo basin, by gold strikes in the Transvaal, by the British occupation of Egypt in 1882, and by German annexations along the east and west coasts, the partition of Africa resembled a frantic and often fatuous race for the spoils left over from previous conquests. The acquisitive powers of Europe divided the dark continent in such formal settings as the Berlin Conference of 1884–85 and in a succession of bilateral treaties after 1890. In Africa itself the partition was marked by confusion, owing to the inaccuracy of maps and the skeletal staffs assigned to occupy and administer these huge territories.[7]

Perhaps the most prominent feature of the new empires was the rise of aggressive competitors to challenge the imperial ascendancy of Great Britain and France. While the Spanish, Portuguese, and Dutch retained portions of their former empires, Belgium, in the person of King Leopold II, followed by Germany and later Italy made successful bids for a place in the colonial sun. And in the Far East the rush for concessions and territories was accelerated by the appearance of three other belligerent powers—the United States, Russia, and Japan. In Europe, after 1870, commercial and industrial rivalries,

---

[6] For further discussion of this controversy see Earle M. Winslow, *The Pattern of Imperialism* (New York: 1948).

[7] R. Robinson and J. Gallagher have examined the "scramble" for Africa at length in their book, *Africa and the Victorians: The Official Mind of Imperialism* (London and New York: 1961). In addition they have contributed a chapter on this subject to *The New Cambridge Modern History*, Vol. XI: *Material Progress and World-Wide Problems* (Cambridge, Eng.: 1962) (ed.), F. H. Hinsley, pp. 593–640.

tensions arising out of the arms race, the increasingly rigid alliance system, and the demands of party politics all contributed to the momentum of overseas expansion. The British empire, furthermore, had a catalytic effect on the Continent where many political leaders and financiers were anxious to match, eventually to surpass, the wealth and prestige of "Greater Britain." Like Spain in the sixteenth century the United Kingdom invited the envy or hostility of every major power. The return to protectionist or neo-mercantilist policies in Europe after 1870 was in large part a reaction to the commanding lead enjoyed by the British in commerce, industry, finance, and empire.

During the 1890's virtually all the great powers showed signs of imperialist hysteria. The perverse application of Darwin's theory of natural selection to nations and societies had created an appropriately amoral environment in which "superior" peoples could prove their fitness to survive at the expense of "inferiors." The advent of mass electorates and of cheap, sensational journalism brought large sections of the working classes into the imperial arena where they could cheer the subjugation of Ashantis, Hottentots, Dervishes, or Bantu peoples. The pioneers and proconsuls of the new empires may have had much in common with the heroes of the old empires. But there was an important difference. In the late nineteenth century a vast audience derived vicarious pleasure from following the exploits of these men in newspapers, lecture rooms, and music halls.

As in the past, religious and humanitarian impulses commingled with material motives. It is easy to scoff at the spiritual factor in the new imperialism, but the fact remains that missionary societies, inspired in many instances by the evangelical movement, were among the first and most persistent agents of European expansion in Asia, in the Pacific, and in Africa. The sense of duty and sacrifice inherent in Rudyard Kipling's invocation to "take up the White Man's Burden" had a genuine appeal to an age less cynical than our own. To argue that the founders of the second empires recognized no higher allegiance than material rewards is to reduce imperialism to only two dimensions.

The new empires were born in an atmosphere of mounting political irrationalism. Fear, no less than greed or sense of duty, produced the so-called new imperialism. In the era of the armed peace (1870–1914) the acquisition of colonies, like the competition in conscript armies and battleships, reflected the collective insecurity of the times as much as it did the self-interests of individuals. Under the stresses of national unification, rapid urbanization, and industrial growth the goals of many political leaders went far beyond the limits prescribed by eighteenth-century statesmen. In Great Britain, France, and Germany, for example, the dependence of the ruling elite on coalition parties for support in domestic and foreign policies served to remove some of the traditional barriers to overseas expansion because ministers were forced to make concessions to many divergent interests as the price of remaining in office. The rapid growth in the 1880's and 1890's of such ostensibly non-partisan organizations as navy leagues, geographic societies, and colonial societies revealed how effectively conflicting interests among their members could be submerged in the cause of empire.

At the same time imperial expansion was not always initiated by the premiers, foreign ministers or colonial secretaries, and pressure groups of the great powers. The stimulus to expand might easily come from the colony or protectorate itself. Native rebellions or the resurgence of Islamism in response to the advent of the white man created the kind of turbulence that led to further expansion.[8] Internal pressures within colonies thus acted to distend empires, often to the dismay of colonial offices in Europe. The broadened bases of political parties together with the dynamics of expansion in overseas territories combined to produce an imperial juggernaut that blinded men to the perils of continued aggrandizement.

II

The second British empire sprang phoenixlike out of the ashes of revolutionary wars in America and Europe. Its growth was as uncoordinated, erratic, and impressive as the expansion of the British economy during the same period. Naval victories against Napoleonic France had enabled the British to improve their position in the West Indies and to increase their exports to the Spanish American colonies. In the Indian and Pacific oceans there was compensation for what had been lost across the North Atlantic; this "swing to the East," as it has been called, concentrated on scattered trading posts and naval stations, for the American experience had discouraged the planting of settlement colonies.[9] Despite the arguments of Adam Smith

[8] See for example J. S. Galbraith, "The 'Turbulent Frontier' as a Factor in British Expansion," *Comparative Studies in Society and History*, II, No. 2 (1960), 150–68.

[9] In this connection see Vincent T. Harlow's classic study, *The Founding of the Second British Empire, 1763–93* (London: 1952).

the expansion of the empire continued apace after 1815. Having won command of the seas, the British were not about to relinquish their naval bases and other holdings overseas in the name of laissez-faire. Although committed in theory to the gospel of free trade, many merchants and industrialists in England tacitly approved or encouraged imperial expansion where their own interests might be involved.

In their important contribution, "The Imperialism of Free Trade," John Gallagher and Ronald Robinson emphasize the continuity of British expansion in the nineteenth century. The crux of their argument rests on the distinction between formal and informal empire. In view of Britain's paramountcy during the mid-Victorian era the pressures for formal annexation of overseas territories were negligible. Once Germany had made her bid for colonies, however, neither Britain nor France could afford the luxury of indecision: fear of annexation by a rival power served as a goad for expansion of formal empire. The occupation of Egypt in 1882—a striking example of the confusion of private and national interests—proved that even Gladstonian Liberals had to countenance aggression in order to safeguard British prestige and the trade routes to India and the East.

Based on the contradiction between liberty and restraint, the British empire was notable both for its aura of innate superiority and for its mosaic pattern. The distinction between white settlement colonies, worthy of responsible government, and native lands or Crown colonies, requiring paternalistic rule, could not be explained away by allusions to autonomy for the latter in the indefinite future. Before 1914 there were few signs, outside the white dominions, that the empire was moving toward the promised land of self-government. What Churchill was to call the "liquidation of the Empire" remained as yet unforeseen.

Arguments against colonial expansion carried more weight in France than in England, for in England the existence of a burgeoning population incapable of feeding itself seemed to make expansion a matter of demographic necessity. To Frenchmen the abundance of resources at home and the fact of a declining birth rate made colonies seem unnecessary luxuries that sapped the vitality of the metropolis. Advances into North Africa in 1830 were greeted with indifference or outright hostility. Despite successive revolutions and bitter factionalism, however, France had acquired by 1870 holdings in Algeria, Madagascar, New Caledonia, Cambodia, and Cochin China. In the last decade of the century apprehension over Germany's increasing strength broke down the remaining obstacles to French colonial expansion. Once converted to colonial imperialism, the French lost no time in creating an elaborate mystique of empire. Implicit in such phrases as *la mission civilatrice* or *l'amitié protectrice* was the assumption of a relationship of mutual advantage. France needed colonies in order to enhance her *grandeur;* the colonies required French manufactures and civilization in order to enter the modern world. Henri Brunschwig discusses the ways in which politicians and publicists justified France's need for colonies in **"The Origins of the New French Empire."**

The most noted French expansionist in the 1880's was the premier whose career is summarized by Thomas F. Power in his chapter, **"Jules Ferry: Imperial Activist."** Like Disraeli in his antipathy to colonies before 1870, Ferry owed his conversion to the writings of imperial publicists like Paul Leroy-Beaulieu as well as to his own instinct for political expedients. In his classic work, *De la Colonisation chez les peuples modernes* (1874), Leroy-Beaulieu argued that colonies were essential to the prosperity of France. The British had erred in the past by founding settlement colonies that did not pay. France, he insisted, ought to establish colonies in those regions most likely to profit both the investor at home and the settler overseas. Ferry used some of these arguments to justify French expansion into Tonkin, Tunisia, and the Sudan. Colonial imperialism, he reasoned, was the "child of the industrial revolution." In the long run his annexationist policies did much to popularize the cause of *France Outremer*.

As in other countries, political and psychological factors played a major role in founding France's overseas empire. Dependence on coalition support and the desire to efface the humiliation of the Franco-Prussian war moved politicians to embrace expansion. The very word empire evoked memories of Napoleonic power and glory. By 1914 *France Outremer* covered almost ten and a half million square kilometers and contained a population of forty-eight million of which only 2.7 percent was French by origin.

The creation of the German colonial empire, analyzed by Mary E. Townsend in the article, **"Commercial and Colonial Policies of Imperial Germany,"** offers another example of the interaction of domestic and external forces in the process of imperial expansion. Faced with the task of building a nation state out of many heterogeneous components, Bismarck soon discovered that timely concessions to important mercantile and financial groups not only strengthened his hand at home but also spread dismay or fear among rival great powers. France and Britain were especially sensitive to German ambitions in Africa. Colonial imperialism thus became a double-edged weapon that was wielded more belligerently after Bismarck's restraining influence had gone. Like the British premier and foreign secretary Lord Salisbury, Bismarck regarded the partition of Africa with dispassion. Both men were sufficiently detached to see through the cant and absurdity of the scramble for "light soil" in Africa. But as statesmen attuned to the requirements of power politics they relied on colonial expansion in order to cope with enemies at home and abroad.

III

Colonial policies varied as widely in the new empires as in the old. Compared with its British or German counterpart, French colonial policy rested on impressive theoretical foundations. Or so it seemed. No matter if the imperial ideology came after rather than before annexation, the French still took great pains to provide their empire with a coherent doctrine. As functional appendages of the metropolis the colonies were supposed to service the needs of the French nation without in any way draining the country's material or human resources. The absence of significant emigration to the colonies—Algeria excepted —gave the empire a unitary form altogether lacking in the British empire. From the outset the colonies were subordinated politically, economically, and culturally to the mother country. Centralization and a penchant for juridical formalism characterized the administration of overseas as well as metropolitan France; and in the minds of most colonial officials the thorough assimilation of the colonies to the mother country took precedence over the elusive ideal of association. However dogmatic they might be about the objectives of empire, the French were as flexible as any other imperial power in the means used to achieve these goals. Hubert Deschamps once asserted that the only constant in French colonial policy was the national temperament—*inconstant, mais universaliste.*[10]

Although British and French colonial policies diverged at many points, it would be a mistake to assume that the two had nothing in common. Both advanced the economic justification of empire, for example. It counted more adherents in England where the perilous imbalance of trade caused anxiety. Although only about one-sixth of British foreign investment between 1815 and 1880 went into the formal

[10] *Les Méthodes et les doctrines coloniales de la France* (Paris: 1953), p. 214.

empire, there were compelling reasons for pegging out claims for the future when the value of colonies might have soared beyond all expectations. In Britain as in France, moreover, the strategic aspects of empire were not overlooked. To fight the war of *revanche* against Germany French militarists relied on the existence of a *force noire* drawn from the colonies; and the English systematically used native levies to conquer and defend India as well as other parts of the empire. The idea of a civilizing mission also permeated both colonial empires. Its spearhead in the nineteenth century had been, in France, the Roman Catholic missionaries supported by the French Navy, and in England, the Protestant missionaries supported by influential members of the evangelical movement.

Many of the differences between the old empires of England and France, on the other hand, carried over into the new. In theory the British still cherished the idea of settlement colonies that would ease the pressure of population and provide the mother country with vital supplies of food and other raw materials. The migration of British subjects and capital to the colonies, even if only a fraction of that to other parts of the world, established ties of a sentimental as well as material nature within the empire. In marked contrast to the French subordination of their colonies, the British regarded their white settlement areas as individual societies with their own lives to lead within the imperial matrix. This pattern of "separate development" derived from the process of transplanting Englishmen and English institutions across the seas. In the non-white colonies, protectorates, and condominiums the dominant note was decentralization. The practice of indirect rule through native chiefs and councils had many precedents before it became official policy early in the twentieth century. The evolution of colonies toward responsible government and eventually dominion status was a long, unsystematic, and often unrewarding process. After the repeal of the Navigation Acts in 1849, for example, Australia and New Zealand carried their fiscal autonomy to the extreme of levying discriminatory tariffs on British goods. This display of independence in tariff policy struck European imperialists as a complete perversion of the proper colonial relationship.

Despite instances of individual brutality and folly the British empire possessed an aura of liberty or constitutionalism that was largely missing in other empires. In the 1830's and 1840's a group of distinguished reformers, led by E. G. Wakefield, Lord Durham, and Charles Buller, had urged the adoption of a systematic colonial policy based on the principle of responsible government or colonial control over purely local affairs. Their efforts marked a new departure in British colonial theory that was epitomized in the famous Durham Report of 1839 advocating limited autonomy for a united Canada. Durham's vision of a federated and self-governing Canada became a reality under the British North America Act of 1867. While the granting of responsible government to Australia and New Zealand in the 1850's may have accelerated the centrifugal forces at work within the empire, these measures of devolution paved the way for dominion status and later the Commonwealth of Nations.

The irony or rather tragedy of British colonial policy is not to be found in the white settlement colonies, but in India and other native lands in the empire. The social exclusiveness of Englishmen toward their non-white subjects, the insistence on a color bar, more than offset the advantages gained through decentralized rule. However devoted the French might be to the idea of colonial subordination, they did not feel the same compulsion to erect insuperable barriers against contact with native peoples. On the contrary, French *colons* and officials were encouraged to study and appreciate native cultures, and their attitude toward miscegenation was indulgent.

Although colonial policies in the German, Belgian, and Dutch empires differed as to time and place, the unifying element was an overriding concern with the economic utility of colonies. Since colonies were meant to be exploited, the chief problem was how to maximize their resources. Efficiency became the trademark of German officials who often approached their tasks with scientific detachment and precision. But even a reputation for brutality in Africa could not disguise the fact that in Samoa and New Guinea the Germans had established what many contemporaries considered model colonies. Their paternalistic programs for native welfare and education compared favorably with those of the British in Nigeria and East Africa.

The view of colonies as objects of exploitation reached one of its extremes in the Belgian Congo where Leopold and his agents deliberately destroyed the traditional culture and society in order to create a submissive working class. This creation of an African proletariat paid such handsome dividends into the royal account that the French were soon applying these methods, although with less success, in Central Africa. As in the past the Dutch continued to prove their adeptness at making colonial imperialism a highly profitable business venture. Their ability to extract wealth from their possessions in South

East Asia was based on indirect rule, a system of modified slavery, and minimal expenditure on colonial administration. Only at the end of the century did the Dutch begin to promote native welfare.

In all the new empires chartered companies played a crucial role in expansion, regulation of trade, and administration. The British East Africa Company, the Royal Niger Company, Rhodes's British South Africa Company, and their many European equivalents represented not only a reversion to old imperial methods but also illustrated the reluctance of governments to commit themselves openly to a forward imperial policy. These *concessionaire* or monopolistic companies wielded extensive powers in the colonies. They supervised trade and production, often owned and used private armies, and influenced or dictated administrative policies.

To some extent every imperial power relied on cheap, compulsory, or slave labor in the hope of making colonies pay for some of their upkeep. It would be both idle and dangerous to generalize about the relative degree of oppression in each colonial empire. If the character of European settlers and district officers varied widely within the same colony or territory, so too did official policy. In dealing with their native subjects no country had a monopoly of virtue and wisdom. Even if the opposite had been true, all the talk of civilizing missions and all the material improvements imaginable would never have convinced the majority of African, Arab, Indian, or Asian peoples that imperialism was much more than a euphemism for exploitation.

IV

This brief survey of European expansion overseas during a span of five centuries gives rise to certain conclusions about the nature and impact of colonial imperialism. However inadequate the perspective of the 1960's for judging this historic process, it is nevertheless possible to see in imperialism the manifestation of Western Europe's world hegemony in this period. The lives of the colonial empires depended upon the ability of five or six great powers in Europe to preserve their political, economic, military, and cultural predominance against challengers from the East and West. Given the failure of these nations to resolve their internal discontents and external differences without resorting to war, it was only a matter of time before their paramountcy passed to the superpowers of the era after World War II. It was the relatively dramatic decline of western Europe through two fratricidal conflicts that made the disintegration of empire inevitable. In the colonies the spectacle of these imperial powers bent on self-destruction irrevocably shattered what was left of the image of Europeans as invincible and infallible. After the First World War prescient men no longer asked whether or not the colonies should be granted independence but when and how. What impeded this emancipation was the presence of renewed and irreconcilable tensions within Europe after 1918.

By the end of the First World War colonial ties were already frayed by the forces of anti-imperialism. Germany emerged from the conflict not only defeated but also stripped of her overseas empire. Like spoils of battle the German colonies were distributed as League of Nations mandates among the victorious powers and associated states. This act of expropriation under the League's auspices supplied new ammunition to the enemies of empire both in Europe and in the colonies, protectorates, and condominiums. Also in the period after 1918 the relationship between Great Britain and the dominions was carefully reformulated in the impressive and ambiguous framework of the Commonwealth. In 1926 an imperial conference in London enunciated the principle of equal status between Britain and the dominions. Five years later the Statute of Westminster (1931) formally confirmed this milestone in the transition from Empire to Commonwealth. Henceforth the dominions, which had heroically proved their loyalty during the war, were to be regarded—in the words of the Balfour Report—as "autonomous communities within the British Empire, equal in status, in no way subordinate to one another in any aspect of their domestic or external affairs, though united by a common allegiance to the Crown, and freely associated as members of the British Commonwealth of Nations." In the same year this flexible political union was given economic substance by Britain's abandonment of free trade and recourse to preferential duties within the Empire.[11]

[11] For a concise study of the Commonwealth and its constitutional framework see Ernest Barker, *The Ideas and Ideals of the British Empire* (Cambridge, Eng.: 1941) and, more recently, K. C. Wheare, *The Constitutional Structure of the Commonwealth* (Oxford: 1960). Standard reference works include the volumes in the *Cambridge History of the British Empire*, 8 vols. (Cambridge, Eng.: 1929–59), Sir Keith Hancock, *Survey of Commonwealth Affairs*, 2 vols. (London: 1937,1942), Nicholas Mansergh, *Survey of British Commonwealth Affairs; Problems of External Policy, 1931–9* (London: 1952) and *Survey of British Commonwealth Affairs; Problems of Wartime Co-operation and Post-War Change, 1939–1952* (London: 1958).

It was the Second World War that gave the greatest single impetus to the disintegration of the new empires. After 1939 and especially in the critical post-war period, colonial ties either ruptured under violent pressure or were redefined so as to preserve the semblance of unity in such loose associations as the British Commonwealth, the French Union (1946), and its successor under the constitution of the Fifth Republic (1958), the French Community. The years since the end of the Second World War have been characterized by a form of imperialism in the East and by decolonization in the West. By establishing satellites in Eastern and Central Europe—a subject too intricately intertwined with other factors to enable us to find space for it here—the Soviet Union not only fulfilled traditional Russian aspirations in these areas but proved that imperialism was no more the highest stage of capitalism than it was of so-called democratic socialism. In the same period the western powers have been trying to prove by deeds rather than words that the Marx-Leninist epithet "imperialist" no longer applies to capitalist societies. The nature of this contraction of European influence and political control and its implications for the future of Africa are discussed by Margery Perham in **"The New Africa Between East and West,"** as well as in our introduction to that concluding article.

The impact of colonization on native or indigenous peoples has taken many forms. The loss of life, the amount of suffering, the irreparable damage done to native cultures—in sum the destructive elements of imperialism—cannot be measured in figures alone. In the volatile area of race relations the expansion of Europe has had lasting repercussions. The smoldering resentment of non-white peoples throughout .the world for having been instilled with a sense of inferiority based on pigmentation is part of the price white men must continue to pay for the ascendancy enjoyed by Western Europe since the age of discovery.

And yet the record of colonization is scarcely barren. Colonial empires have not been founded on negations—to paraphrase Lord Balfour's reference to the British Empire. However traumatic an experience for those at the receiving end, the expansion of Europe overseas has been a powerful agent of what is fashionably called modernization. In other words, colonial status was the price that had to be paid in order to gain admission to the industrial age; and it is as well to remember that every society, without exception, has had to destroy men to build machines. Karl Marx, for example, was quick to see British rule in India in this light. No matter how "swinishly" they might treat the natives, the British were a necessary evil, according to Marx, because their introduction of railways and industry was breaking down the caste system that impeded the creation of a westernized proletariat. By exporting capitalism the British were thus sowing the seeds of its destruction. If Marx's vision was too apocalyptic, his insights into the modernizing effects of imperial rule cannot be ignored. In addition, one must not overlook the constructive aspects of British rule in India and Africa, of the French in North Africa, or the lesser contributions of the Germans in New Guinea and Samoa. The suppression of tribal wars and savage customs, the building of schools, churches, and hospitals, the improvement of communications through road, railway, bridge, and harbor construction, and the development of natural resources must all be taken into account in any final reckoning about imperialism.

Expansion involves a reciprocal process, and the impact of colonization on Europe has taken many forms. The influx of precious metals from the New World affected both politics and society as well as the capitalist economy of Europe; while the representative institutions established in Hispanic America and in the thirteen colonies to the north had important repercussions on Western European polity. Apart from their value to private investors, both the first and second empires served as pawns in the internecine struggles of the old world for power and prestige. Any analysis of the influence of overseas empires on Europe would have to include references to the social, political, economic, cultural, diplomatic, demographic, and psychological facets of each colonizing society. The absence of any consensus about these categories and their contents should serve as a challenge to pursue these studies.

Whether imperialism was good or an unmitigated evil is beside the point. Such judgments belong to the individual conscience. Here we treat imperialism as a fact requiring explanation rather than censure or apology. There is much about this historic movement that remains unknown or open to dispute, not merely in relation to the history of modern Europe but, as we suggested at the outset, to the study of all history. What, for example, has been the role of the human instinct to dominate and be dominated? Is Freud's suggestion correct that dominion over another society—especially the reassurance that there are men inferior to oneself—reconciles us to having to surrender to the demands and discipline of our own society? Or was the "colonial vocation" of

Europeans only the reenactment of childhood fantasies or fears in the
remote villages and plantations of Africa, Asia, and the New World? [12]
Such questions have been asked more frequently in recent years, but
the answers are still in doubt if only because they raise fundamental
and disturbing questions about the nature of man himself.

[12] For an interesting study of the psychological aspects of colonization see
O. Mannoni's "case history" of European and native personalities on the island of
Madagascar, *Prospero and Caliban: The Psychology of Colonization* (London:
1956). The psychology of race and class relations in the British empire is
discussed in Philip Mason, *Prospero's Magic* (London: 1962).

COLONIZATION AND THE MAKING OF MANKIND *

Herbert Lüthy

*Herbert Lüthy, who is a member of the Swiss Federal Institute
of Technology in Zurich, has written perceptively on French political
and colonial affairs. According to Lüthy, the prodigious activity of
Western Europeans since 1450 in transplanting their culture around
the earth has brought about a world revolution. In the article below he
contends that imperial expansion has been responsible for the matura-
tion of non-Western cultures as well as for the cultivation of remote
or uninhabited regions. Colonial empires have come and gone but the
task of breaking down the obstacles to the ultimate integration of
human cultures continues unabated. Lüthy deplores the emotionalism
that pervades most discussions of the colonizing process and insists
that modern civilization and colonization are two sides of a coin that
is more than five centuries old.*

A meeting of historians on "Colonialism and Colonization" certainly raises a terminological problem. Colonization is a great and old
subject of historical study. The word "colonialism," on the contrary,

* Reprinted from Herbert Lüthy, "Colonization and the Making of Mankind." The Tasks of Economic History (December, 1961), *The Journal of Economic History*, Supplement, Vol. XXI, No. 4, 483–95, with omissions, by special
permission of the editors of *The Journal of Economic History*.

seems to me to have come to us from the international rostrums where diplomats and propagandists wage the psychological wars of today; and to my taste it has that Basic English quality of an international vocabulary ready-made for simultaneous translation, where the suggestive power of words is in inverse relation to their accuracy. In its current use it seems to be a synonym of imperialism or, more generally, of domination of one country by another, or by the rulers of another country. But imperialism, at least, says what it means: the policy of building and holding together an empire, a unit of domination which transcends the national state. Foreign domination is a self-defining expression apt to describe all degrees of dependency, from straight political and military to economic or even cultural ones. What, then, is the use of forging yet another term?

Three years ago the Foreign Policy Research Institute of the University of Pennsylvania published a collective study on *The Idea of Colonialism*.[1] I have read it carefully, but could not find what this idea was, or who ever held it. Most of it was an apology for certain forms and aims of bygone colonial policies which, it said, were better than their reputation. If anything, the word "colonialism" seemed to connote this bad reputation of which "good" colonial policies had to be washed clean; an undertaking which, as one critic said, "painfully reminded [one] of those scholarly treatises which seek to show that the divine right of kings was not such a bad doctrine after all." Another part was dedicated to "Soviet Imperialism" and, incidentally, to colonialist ambitions of India, Indonesia, or Egypt; this easily becomes the childish game of throwing a slander back to the slanderer: "Colonialists!"—"Colonialists yourself!" I cannot see what history can have to gain in taking part in that debate.

In Europe, for understandable reasons, not only scholarly, the term has been accepted reluctantly and rather late, but it is now in common use. . . . We might say that colonialism designates certain forms of imperialism or foreign domination which are past and gone, or the last shaky remnants of which are condemned to disappear rapidly—as distinguished from other forms of imperialism and foreign domination which go on prosperously and self-confidently. "Colonialism," I suspect, means foreign domination based on outdated means of power. To confirm this, I looked up the definition of "colonialism" in Funk and Wagnalls' *Standard Dictionary of the English Language*, which gives

[1] Edited by Robert Strausz-Hupé and Henry W. Hazard (New York: 1958). [Editor's note.]

the synonym "imperialism," but also this more explicit meaning: "The policy of a nation seeking to acquire, extend, or retain overseas dependencies." The decisive element in this description is "overseas," and this brings perhaps a clearer technical meaning to the argument. Foreign domination is doomed, I would conclude, when based on naval power; that was successful at a time when the navy was the only arm which permitted far-reaching enterprise with limited forces, and allowed relatively small seafaring countries with small but mobile military forces to control vast oceans and immense coastlines without any possible competition from land powers. It is doomed by new technical developments, such as far-reaching aircraft and missiles, as well as by new ideological weapons which give the same world-wide mobility to what were continental powers with sewed-up sleeves. . . .

If this is the meaning of the necrologies on "colonialism," then we may roughly agree. We can even accept the underlying thesis that continental empires built up by marching armies and kept together by permanent garrisons are more normal phenomena in history than the frail thalassocracies resting on naval power. But then this statement of victory of mass over mobility is free of all moral implications; no one has ever contended that naval empires have been heavier, more cruel or more oppressive than continental ones; the historical record is exactly to the contrary. No doubt the primacy of naval power was an essential feature of what we may call the European era of world history, which starts with Vasco da Gama and Columbus and ends with the end of British rule over the Indian Ocean and its entrances, the succession to which, in spite of the orderly transfer of power in India, is still open. But this story of the rise and fall of naval empires defines only the external framework of colonial history; it does not grasp the emotional impact of the retrospective debate on "colonialism," nor the significance of this imperial past. Throughout history, empires have come and gone, and many have left little more than a trail of ruins; these few, in half a millenium, have changed the structure and appearance of the whole world. More than that, they have created the world in which we live.

The discussion about "colonialism" is concerned with the remnants and hangovers of a colonial past, but ignores what was essential in this past and what remains as its accomplishment: the colonization of the world. I was astonished to see that the American dictionary from which I just quoted the definition of "colonialism" ignores the very term from which it is derived, "colonization"—and this in a country which, in the full sense of the word, was *made* by the most powerful experiment of colonization! This seems to me sadly characteristic of a current way of speaking and thinking which forgets the meaning of words and things and satisfies itself with the debased isms forged by ideologists for smear or praise. The content of the history of colonization is not the rise and fall of colonial empires, the political domination of foreign countries; these have always been transitory. It is, and has been from the beginning of history, the tremendous process by which the world was discovered, opened to man, and settled; the process by which roads, coasts and oceans were made accessible and safe, by which closed continents, forbidden kingdoms and isolated societies were forced open or broken up by new expanding forces, new techniques, new customs, new knowledge, and new forms of social organization. It might be said that the history of colonization is the history of humanity itself. "It is undeniable," as the French *Encyclopédie* stated in 1753, "that all the earth is peopled by colonies." It underlies the whole history of civilizations, which have grown not in stagnant isolation, but only in contact and conflict with other cultures. The word colonization, indeed, means nothing but the spreading of culture, in the great and primitive sense of cultivating the earth; and something of this primitive meaning has survived through all its perversions. There have been ages of magnificent colonization which barely displayed the beginnings of an expansion of political power—the classic example is the Hellenization of the Mediterranean world, which started a process that continued through the Hellenistic states and through the Roman Empire itself long after its original center, Hellas, had been exhausted.

The forces that, time and again, set this process in motion, remain for the most part mysterious. At one spot of the inhabited earth a yeast came into being which raised the heavy dough of mankind and set it in movement, progressing as far as its forces could go; and, time and again, the movement reached its limit and died away in the inert mass. The tremendous outburst of colonizing activity that spread from Europe since the end of the Middle Ages, the voyages of discovery, the search for gold, spices and spoil, the expansion of trade, the religious missions, the emigration of adventurers and dissenters, and the conquests of empire-builders embraced for the first time the whole world. The dynamic of this movement works on, even after the impulse from Europe has been stilled. If ever a chapter in history merited the title of world revolution, it is this gigantic adventure which in a bare half-millennium changed the face of the world unrecognizably, tore entire continents from isolation, transported populations, plants and animal races around the globe, peopled millions of square miles of virgin lands of both hemispheres, and for the first time made it possible to think of mankind as a single whole, and of history as universal history. Even if today, like the sorcerer's apprentice—or like the Greek cities in the Hellenistic age—Europe would often wish the broom back in its corner, still this world revolution has been achieved, and we are all now entangled in this universal history.

This world-wide expansion was one movement, but it proceeded in many forms and in different discontinuous waves. In the vast virgin grasslands of the Northern and Southern hemispheres—North America, Argentina, Australia and Siberia—it took the form of colonization in the primitive sense of the word, and went on with the most astounding success in this country, where a European immigrant society developed free of political control from Europe. . . . In the peopled tropical areas of the world, the first crusading age of discovery sweeping East and West in the fifteenth and sixteenth centuries started in forms quite similar to the crusading kingdoms of the High Middle Ages, as an adventure of soldiers, sailors, nobles, priests and explorers followed by traders, miners and colonization promoters. In the following age of warfare between competing mercantilistic states, an age of colonial wars fought not between Europeans and overseas peoples but among European states, chartered companies, pirates and interlopers themselves, the scattered European trading posts and plantation settlements were again not too different from those of previous Arab, Indian or Malay merchants, and had even more limited influence on the hinterland; as late as the mid-nineteenth century, a James Brooke [2] founding a rajah dynasty in Sarawak strikingly resembles the Arab adventurers who had created their trading kingdoms throughout the Indian Ocean with only a few ships and men, without roots in the land beyond the coast. In Asia as in Africa, it was only the third wave —starting with the Industrial Revolution in Europe—that brought its full impact on the traditional societies of the tropical regions of the Old World, now organized in a haphazard way as complementary parts of a European world factory. After an almost complete interregnum which had made the contemporaries of Marx think of the colonial era as something past and dead, this new lease on life of colonizing activity brought new force into the remnants of the former epochs.

---

[2] Sir James Brooke (1803–68): English soldier and adventurer who became governor and rajah of Sarawak (1841); noted for administrative reforms. [Editor's note.]

Chartered companies flourished anew on the wave of industrial demand and financial speculation, stagnant residues of old slave- or spice-trading posts were suddenly re-awakened and extended, the fever of exploration and even the crusading spirit of the conquistadores were revived in the degraded form of a European civilizing mission. This was the age of European hubris that reached its flamboyant height at the Berlin Congo conference in 1885, when the European powers started the "scramble for Africa" and made it a question of national prestige to plant their colors on every white spot on the map before a rival nation could do the same.[3] Only then did the concept of colonization deviate completely from its meaning. In this race in which all rational, economic or humanitarian motives became mere pretexts, every nation carved out for itself immense unknown territories which, as we now know, they were never able really to colonize, organize, or exploit.

It is this third and last wave of European colonization that has given rise to the theory of colonial imperialism as the last stage, or the last issue, of modern capitalism; a theory which, though its analysis of motivation in many cases is evidently true, is quite incapable of explaining the phenomenon as a whole. It would be more correct to say that colonization and colonial imperialism have been the premises of modern capitalism, which could only develop and grow in the wide open fields of unbridled activities outside the rigid and sterilizing patterns of European state economies stifled by privilege, monopoly and mercantilist regulations. And the decisive fact is that this world-wide economy was created by the very first wave of the European outburst, and in spite of crises and strains was never disrupted again. The crude but efficient chain of exchange which spanned the world from the time of the sixteenth century, set in motion from Europe and in the service of Europe, is now fairly well known in its outlines; its monetary reserves were the silver mines in the Spanish Americas, the harvest of which was brought to Europe with the yearly arrival of the Spanish silver fleets and was drawn out of Spain and of the Spanish Empire by all legal and illegal means of trade, smuggling, piracy and commercial warfare. This Spanish silver, the only valuable merchandise—besides fire weapons and mercenary soldiers—that Europe had to offer in exchange for Asian spice and luxury goods, was brought over in shiploads by the Dutch, English, and French India Companies to the Eastern hemisphere,

[3] The Berlin conference (1884–85) recognized the neutrality and free trade status of the International Association of the Congo and served to intensify the competition for colonies among the great powers. [Editor's note.]

which had drained the European area of bullion since Greek and
Roman times. Columbus' discovery was thus the necessary counterpart
without which Da Gama's new eastern seaway could never have been
exploited.

During three centuries, this West-to-East movement of bullion and
East-to-West movement of goods, converging on Europe, was the fundamental pattern into which all the other complicated and fertilizing
circuits fitted themselves: the trade and manufacture of European countries struggling for their share of the loot against the established monopolies of empires and companies; the subcircuit of the slave trade
from Africa to the West Indies which gave access to the closed Spanish
domain and was the origin of some of the first cheap mass manufactures
for exchange on the African coast; the country trade *"d'Inde en Inde"*
developed by European private merchants between the countries around
the Indian Ocean which lived and mostly still live in isolation from
each other; and finally, on the opposite side of the earth, the South
Sea trade starting with the Manila Ship between Spanish America and
its Far Eastern outpost. The world economy has undergone many revolutions since then, but it was there to stay only a few decades after
the great discoveries of the 1490's, and it is impossible to understand
the development of the modern economy in any of its features without
this groundwork of an already existing world economy. . . . The monetary
systems, the mercantilistic policies, the first experiences in stockjobbing
and credit, all of these grew out of this planetary expansion which
broke up the old patterns of European economies and social structures
long before it disrupted those of the non-European world. In this general view, the Marxist conception of a capitalist system grown up as a
local phenomenon in Western Europe and then, in its last phase, ex-
ploding over the world in the form of colonial imperialism (a concept
which, it must be recalled, was not invented by Marx but by the latter-
day Marxists) is simply history written in reverse.

Nor is this history simply a history of violence; processes of *this*
magnitude are never the work of force alone. However bloody and
cruel many episodes in the history of colonization may be, by and large
the part of force in this world revolution is astonishingly small; it was
with ludicrously few material means that Europe transformed the
world. The empire of the Incas fell in the dust before the attack of a
handful of Spanish adventurers who, on an alien continent as unex-
plored as if it were another star, scarcely knew where they were or what
lay ahead. The immense empire of India was held together to the end

by less than a thousand British police and sixty thousand troops. From the beginning to the end of the history of colonization, we find this grotesque disproportion between the material means of power and the effects produced. This passive capacity of the non-European world to be colonized was as basic a factor in European world power as the European drive for expansion itself. Virtually nowhere did the colonizers come up against political entities and social structures possessing an innate capacity to resist, against peoples who lived in the consciousness of a freedom or independence worth defending, or who cared much if their rulers changed.

As long as the Europeans were simply customers, be it even of slave markets, or nabobs or rajahs not too different from the native rulers and often associated with them, the impact of this European-organized world economy on the non-European societies remained almost negligible, though it was powerful on Europe itself and on the Europeanized Western hemisphere. . . . It was only the introduction of wage payment, together with the increasing impact of Western technology, organization and modes of behavior which, late in the nineteenth century, irremediably broke up the old patterns of tribal or feudal societies, and discredited everywhere the institutions, customs, rites and ways of life of these societies, without offering an understandable and assimilable alternative. All these societies had been perfectly capable of governing themselves in their traditional way of life; very few of them were able to cope with the organizational, technological and social problems created by this contact with a civilization as foreign as a Martian invasion, or able to protect their integrity against the violent or corrupting intrusion of even a handful of Western gold diggers or concession hunters. In this respect, too, the view of European expansion as a series of conquests of weak and peaceful countries by a few imperialist states is a terribly superficial one. Colonization was not primarily the work of governments and states, but of hundreds of thousands of colonists, pioneers, and adventurers, the elite or the outcasts of all European nations. This outburst of surplus energies was the moving force before which the primitive, decaying, or stagnant societies of the non-European world cracked or collapsed.

Political reorganization, and the assumption by individual European powers of the administration of, and therewith responsibility for, the fate of these countries followed as an expression of the need to direct this world revolution along orderly paths and to control the boundless, irresponsible, freebooting and destructive enterprises of pioneers and

adventurers. Only then did constructive and regulating official colonization replace pure mercantilism, which had flung open doors and beaten
down barricades everywhere without regard to the consequences. Colonial administration was in most cases a necessary transition to self-
government under the new conditions of the world, though it was not
always conceived as merely transitional; but in principle, Europeans
always knew that emancipation was its inevitable and in fact desirable
end. . . .

Colonization as the peopling of hitherto vacant or distinctly under-
populated areas has been an irreversible, self-perpetuating process irrespective of political dependence or independence. Colonization as the
ruling of more or less "backward" peoples by foreign managers in the
field of administration, economic exploitation and education, could only
be transitory and had to reach its end either by failure or by its very
success, that is, by growing acquaintance of the dependent people with
the techniques of such management. The end of this sort of colonization might in theory have come by gradual transfer of power to an
educated "native" elite, certainly not without conflicts, resistance and
pressure, but without the violent breakdown which we have witnessed
since the Second World War. Many trends were at work in this direction; British policy in many parts of the Empire acknowledged and practiced the aim of gradual emancipation at a moderate speed which seemed
too slow to the local elites, but which in retrospect seems to have been
fairly adequate to the real development and possibilities of these countries. French assimilation policies, though diametrically opposed in theory to the British concept of self-rule, were less different in practical
working on the spot than first appears. More fundamentally, perhaps,
the classic pattern of the "European world economy," the exchange of
manufactured goods from the Western industrial countries against foodstuffs and raw materials from the backward agricultural countries—
always a trade on unequal terms with a "colonialist" flavor, irrespective
of the political status of its partners—has become more and more obsolete by the transition of Western societies from centrifugal to centripe-
tal expansion, and the corresponding stop to outward demographic
pressure. What economists had always affirmed is now generally recognized: the possession of overseas dependencies, far from being economically vital to the mother countries, is actually a charge. As far as
international relationships between former metropolis and former colonies are concerned, the colonial problem might now be considered as
liquidated. Only in places where, as a product of mixed colonization,

a sizable and firmly settled minority of European origin refuses to climb down to minority status inside a native state, is the conflict insoluble in terms of interstate relations because it is an interior interracial conflict, and where these minorities obtain the backing of their former mother countries, these are the last and heavy stumbling blocks in the way of colonial retreat. But this problem of interracial society, which today is at the bottom of most so-called colonial conflicts and of many others, may arise in quite similar forms for the Chinese minorities throughout Southeast Asia or Indian and Arab minorities on the African shores of the Indian Ocean. It is part of the legacy of *all* colonizations and the biggest challenge to the modern world, which by far transcends the debate on "colonialism" but gives all its venom to it.

The violent breakdown of what was the European world order was brought on by the suicide of Europe in its fratricidal wars of 1914–1945 much more than by any irresistible revolt of the colonized peoples. European power, material as well as moral, was destroyed by the Europeans themselves, and what we might call the colonial counterrevolution was the result much more than the cause of this self-destruction of Europe, which has left behind it the immense power vacuum inside which the new world powers, America, Russia and potentially China now wage their cold or lukewarm wars of propaganda, assistance, and subversion. The principal weakness of many of the new states is explained by the fact that there was neither a gradual emancipation nor an authentically national struggle for liberation—both of which might have been the fruit of colonization having achieved its work—but a sudden collapse of the colonizing power due to reasons entirely foreign to the colonial world. Of all the accusations which are now thrown to their former tutors, the one which is most indisputably true is that these tutors have not, or very badly, achieved their job. This job has now to be finished by weak and ill-prepared governments of populations which can hardly yet be called nations, with the inadequate means they have and the aid they can borrow. For the colonial revolution against Europe (if we like to describe it so) is *not* a counterrevolution against the Europeanization of the world: it is its continuation after the failure of the European powers to achieve it themselves. . . . It is no paradox to say that the colonial peoples have shaken off European tutelage in order to acquire more quickly what their European tutors promised them, but only gave them reluctantly and dilatorily; and it is of little importance if we still call this model of civilization European or give it another name. In all its Western and Eastern variants, it is the form of dynamic social economy, with its acquisitive, egalitarian and efficiency-seeking drive that has spread from Europe and shakes to the bottom all traditional societies that try to attain its material benefits. So, in a different and tortuous way, the work of colonization, with all its shortcomings and failures and its backwash of rancor and bad conscience, has proved irreversible and self-perpetuating, irrespective of the change in political status. Colonization by Europe has come to its end, but the Europeanization of the world, superficial and distorted as it may sometimes appear, is progressing more rapidly than ever.

Most of what I have said is commonplace to all students of colonial history; what I want to stress is this perspective of an all-embracing, irreversible process. The European era of world history can already be seen as a closed chapter. . . . Europe's colonization of the world, as well as all the partial colonizations which preceded it, was neither a chain of crimes nor a chain of beneficence: it was the painful birth of the modern world itself. None of the former colonial peoples remember it with gratitude, for it was alien rule; but none of them wish to turn back the clock, and this is its historical justification. "Colonialism" can be abolished, condemned and outlawed. But if you try to strike colonization from history, you will find that it is not a chapter but the entire book: the tumultuous and frightening genesis of a world which knows for the first time that it is one world and that its compass no longer stops at the edge of the visible horizon. It was a job that had to be done, well or badly, wisely or blindly. As in most human things, it was done rather badly and blindly by men who rarely knew what they did, but by no stretch of mind can we imagine it undone. The history of the "European era" is not simply European history, nor even the history of European hegemony. It is now part of the history of every country of the world. . . .

Many chapters of this immense historical process have still to be written. But in my view they can only be written valuably as parts of the history of the making of mankind in the last half-millennium, and the criterion for the analysis or description of each particular field of colonization might be this: will it fit into the history books of the new states built on these foundations as well as into our own history books? The colonial past of Ghana, from fifteenth-century El Mina [4] down to the British colony and protectorate, is now an integral part of the history of Ghana, exactly as Roman conquest and imperial administration,

---

[4] The site of one of the first forts built (1482) by the Portuguese on the Gold Coast. [Editor's note.]

Germanic invasion and barbarian kingdoms are accepted parts of the history of France; and no Indian historian could think of eliminating the two centuries of British rule from the history of his country. Many chapters of this history are full of ugliness, as are most chapters of history, and attempts at whitewashing are only harmful. . . . To take the most unpleasant example: a comprehensive history of slavery and slave trade in modern times cannot be valuably written as the story of a deplorable but now happily abolished institution, but only as a common history in which Europe, Africa, the Muslim world and the West Indies were taking part, as their history *and* ours. It was an integral part of the political system of large areas of the Muslim world and of the plantation system in the Western hemisphere. It has been part of some of the most permanent structures of African society and has supported the advance of Islamic reigns down to the southwestern shores of the Sahara. It has made great parts of the American continent black, and the abolition of the institution could not cancel its lasting results, which are engraved on the map and in the psyche of man. This too is part of the common history of the modern world and has to be integrated into the consciousness of our past, which alone can make us understand the present. The old philosophical postulate of one universal history has become a practical necessity if we want to drive out the demons of the past, to find a common language which transcends our ideological isms, apologies and acts of prosecution. The era of worldwide colonization has melted all particular histories into one single process of world history in which we are now all entangled for better or for worse. To free ourselves from the bondage of national history, or Western history, or white man's history, and to work at their integration into this one common history of man, is perhaps the historian's part in the task of the modern world, which is the integration of mankind.

SPANISH COLONIAL THEORY AND PRACTICE *

Woodrow W. Borah

Woodrow W. Borah, Professor of History at the University of California, has uncovered many facets of the political, social and economic structure of the Spanish Empire in the New World. In the present study Professor Borah analyzes the interaction of Spanish and Indian cultures as well as the polities of the Crown and the Spanish colonies in America. After tracing the rise of conciliar government in the Indian and Spanish towns of America, he examines the attempts of the Crown to impose a uniform degree of centralization throughout the empire. The clash of interests between popular town councils and an autocratic Crown that opposed autonomous tendencies forms the crux of this article.

The Spanish Empire in America was thoroughly different in development from the Spanish possessions in Europe. Naples, Sicily, and the Netherlands were European states with populations of cultural background at least equal to the Spanish, with the same religion, with systems of law recognized as of equal merit, and with governmental institutions the monarch was sworn to uphold. There could be no massive penetration of such states by Spanish population and customs. Indeed, during the reign of Charles V [1519–56], his subjects could not be certain where the empire had its seat; so that the anger of the Spanish at Charles' Flemish favorites arose more from their fear of colonial status than from annoyance at the painfully generous gifts made from their pockets. It was only in the reign of Philip II [1556–98] that the center of one Hapsburg empire was firmly set in Spain.

The Spanish possessions in America, on the other hand, were acquired by the conquest of populations with stone-age technologies, religions regarded as abominations, and cultures so different that there could be question whether Indians were reasoning men. The new ter-

* Reprinted from "Representative Institutions in the Spanish Empire in the Sixteenth Century: The New World," *The Americas*, XII (1955–56), 246–56, with omissions, by permission of *The Americas* and the author. Copyright by the Academy of American Franciscan History.

ritories were cemented to the Spanish Crown by large-scale immigration of European subjects, wholesale transplantation of Spanish laws and institutions, and thorough-going assimilation of the aboriginal populations. The Leyden burgher of 1570 might resent Spanish interference in traditional local and provincial assemblies; the Quechua Indian of 1570 knew that his life and the lives of his children were irrevocably committed to ways foreign to his forefathers.

The Spaniards did not come to the New World prepared to undertake the profound assimilation of their new subjects. Their own experience in the Mediterranean, and even in the reconquest of the Iberian peninsula, prepared them rather for acceptance of the customs of subject peoples with a minimum of change. But they found the Indian societies too alien in culture and too unserviceable to fit into empire. Aboriginal religions had to be exterminated and replaced by Christianity. Certain customs designated as "unnatural" had to be done away with entirely. Other customs and laws had to be changed to fit into the conceptions of the *Ius Gentium* as it had been formulated by Roman jurists and Christian theologians. The Indian ruling groups had to be reduced to such subjection that any kind of resistance would become impossible. Finally, the Indians had to be brought to provide sustenance for the Spanish settlers in the Indies and revenues for their new monarch.

The pressure of these needs and aims broke down completely the Crown's initial attempts to disturb as little as possible Indian customs and political organization. Its early policy was hopeless in any event since the European settlers had generous ideas of the level of support to which they were entitled from the natives and were better able than the Crown to enforce their views. Moreover, the coming of the Europeans unleashed revolutionary forces within the Indian societies. Alert and aggressive elements among the native ruling groups broke the restrictions of local law and custom to seize privileges and communal land at the expense of the peasantry; men of lesser birth made shrewd use of Spanish law and courts to despoil many of the former rulers and establish a new native nobility on the Spanish and feudal model. It never occurred to the Spaniards to refuse to apply their law or deny access to their courts, however much a jurist like Zorita or missionaries like Motolinía and Mendieta saw that this application made inevitable the destruction of even those parts of Indian tradition and social organization the Spaniards regarded themselves as bound to preserve.

The forces loosed upon Indian life by the conquest thus meant profound change. The impact was made even greater by Spanish decisions to group the natives in compact communities for easier religious care, administration, the securing of labor, and extraction of tributes. The religious and *letrados* [jurists] in their great debate whether to keep the Indians separate from whites or attempt to create a single society, agreed upon this policy of *congregación*. The policy inevitably meant that the new towns must be provided with governments; and, since the Spaniards preferred models drawn from their own experience, that the Indians, although kept separate from Europeans, must live in European-style polity. In Mexico, after some beginnings under earlier administrations, the new, relatively uniform pattern of Indian local government was implanted during the administration of the first viceroy, Antonio de Mendoza, 1535–1551. Each Indian town was administered by native officials: a governor; alcaldes [justices of the peace] usually two, for meting out low justice; regidores or town councillors, usually four unless the town was large or comprised several language groups; at least one constable; and a notary. In addition, there were minor officials for civic and community functions. The governor, alcaldes, and regidores formed the town council. They were elected annually in a meeting in which the local nobility and peasantry were supposed to participate, the election being confirmed by the viceroy, and they were not normally eligible to hold office again for a period, usually of three years. In the course of the sixteenth century, this organization was imposed upon virtually all Indian towns in Mexico, obliterating most of the aboriginal organization. It was implanted almost simultaneously in Central America. Francisco de Toledo, the great viceregal organizer of the South American colonies (1569–1581), established the same pattern with minor modifications in the realms of Peru.

The Indian town governments had extensive powers. They were responsible for public works, maintaining religious worship, administering low justice, providing labor drafts, collecting tributes and payments to caciques [Indian chiefs] and church, and caring for the physical well-being of their people. It is doubtful, however, that we of the twentieth century would call them representative without considerable reservation. Despite all precautions, the Indian nobility usually controlled the elections, to the disadvantage of the peasantry, and illegally maintained the same officials in power for long periods through re-election or rotation of posts. The caciques, whether the old ruling group or a new group rising to power, managed to engross most of the effective power in the towns, and in alliance with the other nobles to exploit the peasantry with a lack of mercy that made even the Europeans wince. Over the Indians there was the Spanish governor of town or province who intervened at will and built up his own extractive system in alliance with the Indian nobility. In short, the new system functioned in much the same way as most sixteenth-century municipal institutions in Europe. There can be no doubt that it provided representation for the effective power in the Indian communities and for geographical and language divisions. Ironically enough, it adhered to the principle of election more than the town governments the Spaniards provided for themselves. The Indian towns did provide orderly and fairly efficient government. Over the centuries of Spanish rule, they brought the Indian populations within the sweep of the new culture and provided an apparatus to replace the lost aboriginal political organization. Furthermore, Indian society was hardly static. In Mexico, where the development proceeded much more rapidly than in Peru, more Europeanized and more alert elements of the Indian population slowly pushed aside the sixteenth-century stratum of caciques. By 1800 Mexico had few caciques within its Indian town governments, and the *cacicazgo* had become an honorary, hereditary institution of minor political and economic value. The Spanish-imposed town structure proved remarkably flexible in encouraging and responding to this development.

Over the great Indian mass lay the new stratum of Spanish immigrants and their descendants, who developed a parallel set of governmental institutions. The immigrants were overwhelmingly of lowly origin in Spain. Over four-fifths of the 150 warriors on Pedro de Valdivia's expeditions to conquer Chile were plebeians by birth, most of them so clearly so that they did not try to claim a better social origin in their petitions for reward from the Crown. But in the New World, the Spaniards found the Indians in firm possession of the lowest places, a possession they had no wish to disturb. The substantial vacancies lay at the top of the social pyramid as clergy, warriors, administrators, and purveyors to the Spanish towns. The result was mass movement upward. The bulk of the Spanish, including townsfolk and merchants, claimed the status of gentry (*hidalgos*) and insisted upon their right to exemption from degrading forms of punishment, to imprisonment only in the form of house arrest, and to freedom from *pechos*—direct taxes which might be collected only from the lowest classes. However much royal officials resisted the colonists' claims, they never dared to try to levy *pechos* in the New World, and because of lack of a standing royal army, they were forced to use the colonists as militia in exactly the capacity the latter claimed should be their principal contribution to the Crown. For all practical purposes, then, there existed only the First Estate, a few titled individuals of the Second Estate, and the topmost ranks of the Third Estate among the Spanish population in the New World, and the Crown in its dealings with them was forced to use the wariness and care it employed with its nobles in Spain.

Among the Spaniards in America, the fundamental form of local political organization was the town. It had been the dominant form in medieval Spain and served effectively as the means of reorganizing and re-Hispanizing the lands of the Reconquest. The settlers brought the Spanish town with them as unquestioningly as they breathed air. Concentration in towns, furthermore, was a necessary form of settlement for a small upper class dominating a large alien population which otherwise could easily pick off isolated families. The Crown itself encouraged the development of towns. It used the claim of the Española settlers that its subjects had a fundamental right to autonomous town organization as a basis for breaching its over-generous grant of political privilege to the Columbus family. In the reign of Philip II, the standing royal regulations provided that Spanish settlement be in towns.

The development of Spanish towns in America was remarkable. At the time of the conquest and settlement of the New World, the towns in Spain had lost much of their earlier vigor; royal intervention had destroyed most local autonomy; and concentration of power in the hands of an increasingly smaller group within the town populations had deprived town governments of their earlier broad popular base and the invigorating participation of large groups in public affairs. In the New World, where white settlement began far in advance of the reach of royal authorities and beyond their power to meet emergencies, there was necessarily a revival of the earlier vigorous, medieval Spanish town life. The towns cared for the well-being of their settlers with a thoroughness unknown in Spain. Some of the early towns, especially on the mainland, exercised almost sovereign attributes. They raised armies, appointed and deposed royal captains and governors, raised funds, prepared campaigns of defense and conquest, and administered the royal justice. The council of Mexico City in its first years granted lands to settlers over the length and breadth of Mexico.

Many of the towns rapidly developed elective and consultative features that insured firm control by the townsfolk at large even though the first council of almost every town was appointed by the governor of the district or by the head of the conquering expedition. Under a decree of Charles V, issued in 1523 and incorporated in the Laws of the Indies in 1680, the burghers were entitled to elect their councillors unless the royal contract with the leader of the conquest provided otherwise. Most of the towns of Cuba and the Río de la Plata each year elected not only their councillors but also other town officials by what amounted to suffrage of all free men. Furthermore, even where the council was appointed, the members had to be burghers, and usually there were so few burghers that it was difficult to find enough to serve. In the early towns, composed as they were of fighting men, no council could hope to function unless it had the approval of the burghers.

A number of customs which became prominent in the New World further strengthened popular control over the town councils. For decisions on important questions, the councils in many areas invited prominent citizens to sit with them to assure that the problem would be fully discussed and the decision the one truly desired by the burghers. This was the *cabildo ampliado*. The culmination of popular control was reached in areas like the Río de la Plata where important questions were decided by calling all the townsfolk together in the "open" *cabildo* [*abierto*.]

Such wide popular control was obviously as distasteful to the Crown as the autonomy of the medieval towns in Spain. As fast as the Crown extended government by its own bureaucracy to the conquered areas, it began to make substantial breaches in municipal privileges. Royal governors reviewed the decisions of the town councils and successfully asserted the right to participate in sessions. Other royal officials resident in towns, especially treasury agents, also secured the right to participate. The elective principle was breached by the Crown at will by appointing permanent councillors, either as a reward for past services or as return for suitable donations to the treasury. After the establishment of viceregal governments, the viceroys made good their powers to supervise town governments. The long-term royal policy was to curb a dangerous autonomy, which was made even more so in the middle of the sixteenth century by the emergence of the conquerors and their sons as local aristocracies controlling the councils of the larger towns and asserting claims to special treatment through them. To meet this danger the viceroys upheld at once the right of the Crown to intervene and the right of other burghers to participate in town government in whatever spheres the Crown left to the townsfolk. Perhaps the most notable instance of such action was Toledo's victory over the conqueror aristocracy of Cuzco. In general, a rule of distance operated in the success of royal assertion of control. The towns which were seats of royal, especially viceregal administration, or near such seats suffered severe losses of autonomy; those at a considerable distance from the viceroys and audiencias retained far more of their earlier autonomy; those on an open frontier as in the Río de la Plata retained virtually undiminished autonomy and popular control. Even where the Crown successfully imposed substantial curbs on the towns, however, they retained a great deal of their original vitality. Permanent councillors were townsfolk, living in the town. They might have demands for private enrichment but they also had to represent the broader town interests if they wished to continue living in it. The town councils, whatever the method of selection of their members, served as centers for the formulation of demands upon the Crown and resistance to increases of taxes and extensions of royal authority. As far as the upper groups among the Spaniards were concerned, then, there was effective representation in virtually all towns despite royal inroads.

Royal distrust of formal representative institutions for its white subjects extended to all attempts to establish regional bodies. Legally the Spanish dominions in America were realms of the Crown of Castile, but distance made it impossible for American subjects to be represented in the Cortes of Castile. There was no formal Second Estate in the New World during the sixteenth century, but the constitution of the Castilian Cortes after 1538 as a body solely of the Third Estate could have been applied in the convocation of Cortes for America or each of the vice-royalties in America. This was never done. Royal governors did convene assemblies. In 1518 the Jeronymites administering Española called a meeting of representatives of the cities, carrying out their instructions to consult wise and experienced settlers. In 1525 there was a similar meeting of town delegates in Mexico; in 1528 another in Cuba. But all of these meetings were described by the royal governors as consultative, the term Cortes never being used. Without formal royal summons and the presence of sovereign, regent, or viceroy, there could, of course, be no Cortes. Mexico City in one vice-royalty and Cuzco in the other obtained formal royal grants assuring their primacy among other cities in assemblies, but in both instances the royal grant carefully avoided the term Cortes and added that without express royal summons there was to be no assembly. The caution of the Crown undoubtedly reflected the fear of popular institutions after the Comunero civil war in Spain and the frightening experience of almost losing Peru in the 1540's.

Nevertheless, the major function of the Cortes in Castile and Aragon, in the eyes of the sovereign, was to furnish grants of money, and as the government of Philip II went through its first bankruptcy in 1557–1559, that cautious monarch was driven to think of using the same device to extract further revenues in the New World. In 1559 the instructions to the Count of Nieva and his fellow commissioners sent to Peru to examine the question of permanent encomiendas, suggested that they consider convoking Cortes to get a grant for the king. The Cortes, if called, were to be for that one purpose. Nieva and his commissioners apparently considered conditions in Peru too turbulent to make the experiment. A similar inquiry by the Marqués of Falces in New Spain in 1567 encountered the difficulty that the council of Mexico City, although willing to have the proposed Cortes vote funds for the king, demanded that such grants be coupled with redress of grievances. The demand from a realm which was then under investigation of rebellion was enough for Philip II to abandon any further discussion. Other proposals to hold assemblies of colonial delegates all foundered upon the same distrust. . . . Despite the royal bankruptcies of the sixteenth and seventeenth centuries, the Crown bureaucracy never dared resort to assemblies, whether dignified by the name of Cortes or not, for securing additional revenue. In consequence, such was the Spanish sense of legal requirement and the Crown's respect for tradition, that although indirect taxes customary in Spain could be imposed and rates raised, the Crown could not levy direct taxes. The nearest equivalent it could resort to was a public plea for voluntary gifts, the *donativo gracioso* as against the *servicio*.

The Cortes had a second function; it was a means by which the monarch might ascertain the opinions of the influential groups in his kingdom. This was a function which petition alone could not fulfill as the Crown was made painfully aware by revolts in Peru and threats of revolt elsewhere when, with the New Laws of 1542, it attempted to impose a reform repugnant to the bulk of the Spaniards. A substitute of sorts arose as cities in the same province found it necessary to consult each other on matters of mutual concern and sought to pool the expense of sending agents to treat with the king and the Council of the Indies. . . .

The favored solution of the royal bureaucracy involved return to the basic idea out of which had developed the medieval Estates-General: the obligation of the sovereign to seek council and of his subjects to give it. Royal governors in America on royal instruction very early adopted the practice of asking the advice of prominent and experienced members of the community. The men were invited to submit their opinions in writing as individuals or at most after consultation of a small group without any constitution of a formal body. The practice was soon enlarged to involve consultation of spokesmen for any significant group which might be affected by proposed legislation. Decision, however, always lay with the Crown, which merely wished to make certain through long consultation and careful examination of vested interests that the legislation would be the most widely acceptable to its subjects, particularly those who counted, and would provoke the least possible disturbance. Slow and cumbersome though this system of consultation was, it proved remarkably effective. There can be no doubt that it helped give stability to Spanish administration in the New World and, within the medieval conception of social classes, provided full expression for the opinions of the population on all major problems.

These, then, were the adaptations of civil European representative institutions as they developed in Spanish America in the early and middle parts of the sixteenth century. I have omitted the trade guilds which developed as in Spain but had no direct participation in the town councils, and the First Estate, which developed its own councils and capitular assemblies for church matters. It is clear that the implantation and modification of representative institutions proceeded in two major phases. The first could be described as the Crown in pursuit of subjects who were enjoying in the New World a freedom that was rapidly being destroyed in the Old. In most areas in this initial phase, the Spanish conquerors brought the Indians into subjection with little, if any, help from the Crown. They operated under formal contracts with the Crown or under a general obligation of subjects to extend their prince's dominions. Royal organization was rudimentary at best; such royal agents as were present regarded themselves rather as conquerors and imposed few limits upon their companions. The conquerors almost invariably conducted themselves as loyal subjects however, and, applying the precedents of the Reconquest in Spain, founded towns and usually accepted royal governors with little demurrer. Under the same precedents, they also attempted to set themselves up as a feudal aristocracy, holding the Indians in fief and claiming a monopoly of local offices. Their ideas were in the feudal pattern of the fifteenth century and were reasonable enough. But the Crown which was fighting to curtail feudal privilege and end local autonomy in Spain, regarded the conquerors' ideas and claims not merely as old-fashioned but actually as seditious.

This initial phase, incidentally, was usually characterized by merciless and unchecked exploitation of the Indians with little attempt at any enduring reorganization of Indian political and social structure.

A second phase began when the Crown set out to establish effective royal government in the newly won areas. This was a slow process, varying in time from region to region. The Crown built up an administrative group in each of the major centers recruited from the hungry younger sons of the higher nobility in Spain and from men trained in Roman law with its conceptions of the omnipotence of the prince. With the help of a great inflow of settlers who objected to the conquerors' pretensions to monopoly of local office and attempted preemption of lands and labor, the royal bureaucracy sharply curbed the new feudalism and broke the power of the conquerors. In Mexico the last dangerous opposition ended in the 1560's with the suppression of the so-called conspiracy of the second Marqués del Valle (Cortés' son, Martín); in Peru merciless execution and exiling of the openly rebellious consolidated the royal power by the 1570's. Political life in Spanish America was brought under a royal control which was characterized by a degree of absolutism greater than that achieved in Spain but tempered almost invariably by consultation and careful respect for vested interest.

A third period in the development of royal intervention began in the second half of the sixteenth century as a result of the financial straits of the monarchy. Between bankruptcies Philip II tried desperately to find new sources of revenue. One of his most fateful expedients was the sale of public offices. In 1559 notarial offices in America were ordered sold to the highest bidders at public auction although only men of notarial training might hold them. During the next thirty-five years numbers of other offices were put up for sale. In 1591 posts in the Spanish towns, including seats on the councils, were declared subject to sale by the Crown and there began not merely the preemption of existing posts by the Crown for revenue but also a vast increase in the number of posts. Philip II was careful to restrict these sales to fee and municipal offices and reserve the salaried posts of royal justice and administration so that the Crown would retain a trustworthy bureaucracy. Under his successors even these offices were put up for sale, the posts of viceroy and judge of the audiencias in general continuing to be exceptions.

The results of this systematic sale of offices were a great apparent extension of royal authority as municipal posts and local offices of almost all descriptions were taken over by the Crown. Another and more enduring effect, which became clearly apparent under the successors of Philip II, was the loss of the Crown's control over its own bureaucracy, for the official who had bought a post had an undeniable life interest in it and the right to nominate his successor in return for another payment. The bureaucracy in all but its highest reaches became the possession of propertied men, mostly Spaniards born in America and, to a lesser extent, immigrants from Spain. A vast network of interest came into being, flexible enough to admit newcomers with enough power or proper qualifications to claim a place at the trough, tenacious enough to resist efforts at displacement for two centuries, and effective enough to drain the revenues of the empire, leaving rather little for the imperial government in Madrid. Without recourse to a formal device for representation, Spanish America thus achieved in large measure the end sought in Europe by the great revolutionary movements of the sixteenth and seventeenth centuries: the direction of the state by the new wealth.

THE PORTUGUESE IN BRAZIL *

Charles R. Boxer

Charles R. Boxer is author of numerous books about the expansion of Europe in the sixteenth and seventeenth centuries. Such works as The Christian Century in Japan, 1549–1650 (Berkeley, Calif.: 1951) *and* The Dutch in Brazil, 1624–1654 (Oxford: 1957) *have attracted the general reader as well as the specialist. In his book,* Salvador de Sá and the Struggle for Brazil and Angola (London: 1952), *Boxer describes the rise and decline of a family that helped to guide the fortunes of Brazil for four generations. The last member of this distinguished oligarchy to govern Rio de Janeiro, Salvador de Sá (1602–1686?) played a prominent role in safeguarding the Portuguese empire against rebellion and the overt threats of European rivals. The following selection, however, does not deal with the story of his life, but with conditions in Brazil at the turn of the sixteenth century.*

* Reprinted from Salvador de Sá and the Struggle for Brazil and Angola (London: 1952), pp. 1–3, 11–17, 36–37, 388–89, with omissions, by permission of the Athlone Press. Copyright, 1952, by the Athlone Press.

The common Portuguese objection to Spanish matrimonial alliances which is reflected in the proverb "de Hespanha nem vento nem casamento" ("neither wind nor marriage from Spain") is largely derived from a recollection of Philip II of Castile, "the devil of high noon," whose mother and first wife were Portuguese princesses.[1] His descent from the house of Aviz enabled Philip to claim the crown of Portugal when the succession thereto was disputed on the death of the decrepit Cardinal-King Henry, in 1580. His claims, legal and otherwise, were enforced with the aid of Alva's veterans and Mexican "silver bullets," in a judicious combination which enabled him to boast of his new domain, "I inherited it, I bought it, and I conquered it."

From 1580 to 1640, Spain and Portugal formed a dual monarchy, somewhat on the lines of England and Scotland in 1603–1702. By agreement between the Spanish monarch and the Portuguese Cortes (or Parliament) of Thomar, which in 1581 formally legalised Philip's seizure of the Portuguese throne, the two countries and their respective colonies were to be administered on an exclusively national basis, as hitherto. Thus Portugal in theory, and her colonies in practice as well as in theory, retained administrative independence during the personal union of the two crowns in the kings of the Spanish branch of the Hapsburg dynasty. Although the contrary is usually alleged, the Spanish kings scrupulously respected this agreement for the first few decades of this regime, often to the detriment and in face of the loud complaints of their original subjects. Spanish-American colonial officials frequently complained that whereas the Portuguese would not tolerate any Castilians in their overseas territories, Portuguese merchants, and even settlers, swarmed throughout the viceroyalties of Mexico and Peru. Nevertheless, the union of the two crowns was not popular in the smaller country, where it was later dubbed the "sixty years' captivity" in allusion to the period of Jewish exile in Babylon.

The papal bull of 3 May 1493, and the treaty of Tordesillas (1494) by which Spain and Portugal agreed to amend it, had, in effect, divided the non-European world into the respective spheres of influence of the two countries. The dividing line was a meridian 370 leagues west of the Cape Verde islands, Portugal being supposed to confine her discoveries and expansion to the east of this line, and Spain to the west,

[1] Philip II (1527–98): only son of Emperor Charles V and Isabella of Portugal; King of Spain (1556–98); militant champion of Counter-Reformation, he launched the "crusade" against England in which the Armada was defeated (1588). [Editor's note.]

until (presumably) they met on the opposite side of the globe. In 1580, the king of Spain's Portuguese inheritance was no mean thing, but Brazil was not then its brightest jewel. The first of modern colonial empires began with the conquest of Ceuta from the Moors in 1415, and the discovery and settlement of Madeira and the Azores followed before the death of Prince Henry the Navigator in 1460.[2] The West African coast was thoroughly explored in the next thirty years, trading settlements being established at various points. In the decades following the opening of the Cape route to India in 1498, the Portuguese founded a chain of fortified posts and commercial colonies extending from Sofala in East Africa to Macao on the shores of the South China sea. This holding of the gorgeous east in fee was what attracted King Philip and aroused the cupidity of his Protestant enemies; but the Brazilian agricultural settlements, although less coveted than the entrepôts of the orient, were rapidly growing in importance.

Historians still argue whether the discovery of Brazil by the Portuguese in May 1500 was accidental, and whether they had been preceded by the Spaniards. Cabral[3] had christened his new-found land "Terra de Vera Cruz," but the invocation of the true cross soon gave way to the more mundane name of Brazil. This word was derived from the ruddy colour of the indigenous dyewood which resembled a live coal (*braza*), and which formed the country's principal export for about four decades. During this time, the French frequented the Brazilian coast almost as much as did the Portuguese, who eventually realised that they must make greater efforts if they wished to retain and expand their few footholds along the littoral.

In the fifteen-thirties, King John III of Portugal [1521–57] divided the Brazilian coast between the Amazon and São Vicente into twelve captaincies (*capitanias*) which were granted to proprietary landlords known as *donatários*. Their rights and privileges roughly corresponded to those of the "lords proprietors" who later settled some of the English colonies in the Antilles and North America. The *donatários* were required to settle and defend the land at their own cost, receiving

[2] Prince Henry of Portugal (1394–1460): called Henry the Navigator for his life-long devotion to the study of exploration and navigational aids; third son of King John I; revered patron of maritime expeditions; established observatory and school of navigation, thereby accelerating Portugal's expansion overseas. [Editor's note.]

[3] Pedro Alvares Cabral (1460?–1526): Portuguese navigator who discovered Brazil reputedly by accident in April 1500 while en route to the East Indies. [Editor's note.]

in return extensive administrative, fiscal and judicial powers over the colonists whom they induced to emigrate to their respective captaincies. Owing to the superior attraction of the "easy money" and glittering luxury of the Asian settlements, few of the wealthy nobility showed any interest in the Brazilian venture, and most of the grants were taken up by ordinary *fidalgos* or gentry. Since none of these were rich enough to provide adequate capital for such costly undertakings, four of the original grants were never settled by their *donatários*, and another four succumbed to attacks by hostile natives. King John III soon realised that it was necessary to establish a central authority if the remaining settlements were to be saved from collapse. Accordingly, Thomé de Sousa [4] was sent out as governor-general, with orders to establish the seat of the government at Bahia de Todos os Santos (the Bay of All Saints), in 1549. He was accompanied by six members of the recently founded Society of Jesus, fit representatives of the religious order which was to play such an important part in the growth and development of colonial Brazil.

.   .   .   .

When the young Salvador [5] first went to Brazil with his grandfather and namesake in 1614, the colony was already on the high road to prosperity, although it had not yet attained a position comparable with that of Mexico and Peru. It is interesting to contrast the Portuguese methods of colonisation in South America with those of their Spanish neighbours. Generally speaking, the Spanish effort was much the more systematic of the two. The Castilian conquistadores sought out the healthy highlands of the interior, deliberately selecting areas which were favourable for white colonisation. The Portuguese, on the other hand, for long confined their activities to the tropical coastal belt. Their efforts were not so carefully directed by the government at Lisbon as were those of the Spaniards by the authorities at Madrid— but then neither were they so hamstrung by over-centralisation. In connection with the penetration of the interior, Brazil's first native-born historian, Frei Vicente do Salvador, writing in 1620, makes an oft-

[4] Sousa was a personal friend of King John III and a cousin of Martim de Sousa, the admiral who commanded the first colonizing expedition to Brazil (1530–33). [Editor's note.]
[5] Salvador de Sá (1602–86?): great grandson of Mem de Sá the third governor general of Brazil, governor of Rio de Janeiro (1637–43, 1648, 1660–62); governor of Angola (1647); appointed general of the Brazil fleets (1644). [Editor's note.]

quoted camparison between the Portuguese in Brazil, who were satisfied with sidling like crabs along the coastline from one sugar-plantation
to another, and the Spaniards who pushed so rapidly and so far
into the hinterland in their search for mines.

The chief reason why the Portuguese settlements clung to the coast
for so long was an economic one, but it was powerfully reinforced
by geographic factors. Sugar was the principal crop from which the
colonists hoped to make their fortunes, whereas it was silver-mines like
Potosí and Zacatecas that formed the principal attraction for Spaniards
emigrating to the New World. Sugar had been introduced into Brazil
from Madeira and São Thomé, having been transplanted from Sicily
to the former island through the efforts of Prince Henry the Navigator
a century earlier. The first permanent settlements in Brazil therefore
took the form of sugar-plantations, which were centred around the
engenho or mill for grinding the cane and preparing the sugar. The
engenho was more economically operated by water-power than by
oxen, so a site near a river was preferred. The brazilwood, valued as a
dye, had been a royal monopoly from early times. Its exploitation was
leased or farmed out by the crown on relatively easy terms. Hides,
tobacco and cotton were other articles of export by the second decade
of the seventeenth century, although the bulk of the cotton production
was consumed locally.

For the export of all these goods to Europe, easy access to water and
to ocean-going shipping was essential, in order to reduce the cost and
the difficulty of haulage through the hills and the bush. Hence the
original settlements naturally tended to be laid out near the mouths
of rivers and at natural harbours along the coast. There was no reason
to move them much further inland, since none of the rivers between
the Amazon on the north and the Rio de la Plata on the south were
navigable for any great distance, being blocked by boulders, cataracts,
or rapids within less than a hundred miles from the sea. The roads and
tracks made by the Incas and the Aztecs in Peru and in Mexico greatly
facilitated Spanish penetration of those countries; but Brazil was
inhabited by wandering forest tribes in the neolithic stage of civilisation, whose footpaths through bush and jungle did not afford the same
help to man and beast. . . . In Brazil itself, nearly all communication
between the different settlements along the littoral was made by sea,
overland contacts being difficult, few and far between.

The early exploitation of gold- and silver-mines by the Aztecs and
the Incas further helped the Spaniards to penetrate and settle the in-

terior, by attracting people away from the coast in search of these precious metals. Moreover, the Spaniards came to America with considerable experience of working metals in their homeland, particularly in the Biscayan provinces with their wealth of iron ore. The Portuguese, on the other hand, were so short of mining engineers that a government official complained in the sixteen-thirties that there were not four men in Portugal who knew how to prospect for mines or to work them when located. This was probably an exaggeration; but it is significant that nearly all the professional miners of whom we hear in Brazil during the seventeenth century (other than those who worked placer mines and gold-diggings) were foreigners—Spaniards or Germans.

For these and other reasons, the Portuguese government tended to be satisfied with the exploitation of Brazilian agricultural wealth, in the form of sugar, brazilwood and tobacco along the coastal zone. It left the exploration of the interior to private enterprise, which took the form of long-distance slave-raids organised by a race of peculiar half-breeds, variously called *Mamelucos, Paulistas,* or *Bandeirantes.* . . .

Colonial Brazilian life and civilisation had from the beginning a markedly rural stamp. Once the Indians had been enslaved in or driven away from the immediate neighbourhood of the coastal settlements, the plantation owners lived on their estates and only visited the towns periodically to attend religious services and *festas.* The principal Brazilian settlements, Bahia, Olinda, and Rio de Janeiro, were mere villages in comparison with Mexico City, Lima, and Potosí. Nor did the trade-guilds in Brazil ever achieve a status comparable with those of Peru in the colonial period. This may have been partly due to the fact that Brazil, even more than Spanish America, depended on slave-labour for its existence.

In one way, the union of the Spanish and Portuguese crowns in the persons of the Spanish Hapsburgs accelerated the development of Brazil. Large numbers of enterprising persons who did not like the Spanish yoke at home emigrated to the colony where it was purely nominal. Brazil was a favourite place of refuge for the persecuted crypto-Jews or *Christãos-novos* (new Christians), since the Inquisition did not maintain a branch in the colony (as it did in Portuguese India and Spanish America) but contented itself with the occasional dispatch of visiting commissioners. These itinerant commissioners seem to have been surprisingly moderate individuals on the whole. No *auto da fé* was celebrated in Brazil during the seventeenth century, in great contrast to the activity of the Holy Office in Mexico and Peru. . . .

The emigration from Portugal to Brazil was of a far healthier and more balanced type than that to the East, which, as far as mere numbers went, still seems to have exerted a superior attraction for the unattached male. But whereas the lubberly East India carracks took from six to nine months on the voyage from Lisbon to Goa, where they often arrived with the loss of half their passengers and crew, the Brazil voyage was normally a matter of weeks, and was made in smaller and less crowded ships. Not only was the mortality rate correspondingly insignificant, but whole families often emigrated to Brazil, whereas only soldiers and unmarried men (or at any rate men without their wives) were normally embarked for India. The superiority of the married man over the bachelor as a potential coloniser was recognised from early times. The Jesuits urged that girls (even those of bad character) should be sent out to marry. One experienced colonial official reminded King John III that "one married man is worth ten bachelors here; for where the single men only try to get away, the married men strive only to develop the land and to live on it."

Convicts or *degredados* were often sent from Portugal to the Asian, African, and American settlements in the sixteenth and seventeenth centuries, exile to the colonies being one of the most frequent forms of commutation of the death penalty. Complaints of this practice were loud and frequent from colonial officials; but it must be remembered that (as was the case with Australia in the early nineteenth century) many of these involuntary pioneers were not necessarily hardened criminals, but were exiled for what would nowadays be regarded as minor peccadillos. We have no reliable figures for the emigration from Portugal to Brazil over any considerable length of time, but judging from the rapid growth of the white colonial population in the last quarter of the sixteenth century, it must have been quite respectable. Many families came from Madeira and the Azores, where over-population was particularly acute, while the seafaring communities of Vianna do Castello and Aveiro in northern Portugal provided a good quota. It may be estimated with a fair degree of probability that in the year 1612 there were about fifty thousand settlers of European origin (but not necessarily of unmixed European blood) in Brazil. Nearly half of these were concentrated in the north-eastern captaincy of Pernambuco which was the richest sugar-producing district.

Brazil at this period can fairly be described as prosperous. Some two hundred sugar-mills provided an article of export which was becoming increasingly popular in Europe, despite the crippling taxes imposed on it at Portuguese ports. The colony as a whole yielded more money to the home government than it cost in administrative and defence expenditure, whereas the Asian possessions were a heavy financial liability to the crown.

.   .   .   .

The home government controlled the colony through the medium of several councils and tribunals which had their headquarters at Lisbon. From 1604 to 1614, the chief of these was the *Conselho da India,* or India Council, which was apparently founded by King Philip III (II of Portugal) [1598-1621] in imitation of the *Consejo de Indias,* which had directed the destinies of Spanish America since 1524. Despite its name, the Portuguese India Council was not restricted to Asian affairs, but handled African and Brazilian matters as well. This innovation aroused much opposition from the older tribunals which had previously shared the supervision of the *conquistas* ("conquests") as the overseas dominions were officially termed, and which resumed their former functions on the abolition of the *Conselho da India* in 1614. The two principal tribunals henceforth concerned with the colonies were the *Mesa da Consciencia e Ordens* and the *Conselho da Fazenda.*

The Board of Conscience and [military] Orders dated from the reign of King John III, and advised the crown on matters of high ecclesiastical and religious policy in Portugal and its overseas possessions. It made recommendations regarding the disposal of church livings and benefices, including the selection and appointment of bishops. It was also concerned with the collection and administration of tithes in the colonies on behalf of the crown, with the religious holdings of the three military orders, with the ransom of captives from the Barbary corsairs, the moral justification of the Negro slave-trade, and so forth. It acted, in short, as the keeper of the king's conscience on affairs of state. The Board consisted of a number of ecclesiastical and civil lawyers under the presidency of some great noble or prelate.

The *Conselho da Fazenda,* or Revenue Council, dealt primarily with financial concerns, as its name implies. It was also responsible for the outfitting of the East India fleets, and exercised a general supervision over the trade with the Asian, African and Brazilian settlements. It was normally composed of three noblemen who were councillors of state, three civil lawyers, and four clerks. There was inevitably a good deal of overlapping between the *Mesa da Consciencia* and the *Conselho da Fazenda,* while the Council of Portugal, which represented the national

interest at Madrid, also concerned itself with matters of high colonial
policy, but its function was purely advisory.

. . . .

The century of Brazilian history which opened with King Philip's
seizure of the Portuguese throne in 1580, and closed with the founda-
tion of the colony of Sacramento on the banks of the Rio de la Plata
in 1680, might well be termed "the century of sugar." The Pernambuco insurgents of 1645 aptly chose "sugar" as their password, and
"slaves" would have been the logical countersign had they needed one.
The sugar-trade and its corollary the slave-trade were the two pillars
on which Brazilian colonial society was built during this its formative
period.

Despite the economic crisis of the sixteen-seventies and eighties,
Brazil at the time of Salvador's death was in a more settled and flour-
ishing condition than at the time of his birth. Portuguese sovereignty
ran in fact, as well as in name, from the mouth of the Amazon to the
Rio de la Plata. The various coastal settlements were in closer touch
with each other than they had been at the beginning of the century,
much of the hinterland had been explored, and the Paulistas had trav-
elled overland to Grão Pará. The central administration was functioning more effectively, and an episcopal hierarchy had been established
with an archbishop at Bahia. The Jesuits could boast that their Brazilian
colleges were on a level with those of Europe, and an increasing number of colonial youths went to Portugal to complete their education at
Coimbra. Peasant immigration from northern Portugal and the Azores
continued at a steady rate, and a considerable number of colonial office-
holders settled in Brazil on the expiration of their terms. The slave-trade
with Angola flourished, whatever twinges of conscience those who were
connected with it may occasionally have had. Indian slaves had been
almost entirely replaced by Negroes, save in Pará, the Maranhão, Ceará,
and São Paulo. If Pernambuco had not quite recaptured the exceptional
prosperity which it had enjoyed in the decades before the Dutch invasion of 1630, Bahia and Rio had both increased in size and prosperity.
The colonial municipal councils often acted as something more than
the guardians of the selfish interests of the sugar-planters, or as opponents of the "liberty of the Indians"; and their representations to the
crown on matters affecting the public weal were often (though not
invariably) well received at Lisbon.

On the debit side, the colonists had good reason to complain of the
economic difficulties caused by the monopolies of the Brazil Company,

and of the perpetuation of the convoy system after the strategic necessity
for it had ended with the peace of 1668. The imposition of heavy taxes,
originally levied to meet sudden demands on the treasury, as for the
dowry of Catherine of Braganza and the indemnity to Holland in
1661–3, but then maintained for years (or even centuries) for purely
Portuguese interests, naturally caused a good deal of discontent. Slave
rebellions were a perpetual menace in some areas, particularly in Pernambuco and Bahia, where the escaped Negroes gathered in forest
settlements called *quilombos,* whence they raided outlying farms and
plantations, Yellow fever was introduced into Brazil about this time,
and there were periodic ravages of plague at Pernambuco and elsewhere. But despite these and other drawbacks, the history of Brazil
during the seventeenth century was one of consolidation and progress.
The pioneer days of the sixteenth century were over. The formation of
a nation had begun.

COLONIES AND THE MERCANTILE
SYSTEM *

Hugh E. Egerton

*For many years Hugh E. Egerton (1855–1927) was one of the ac-
knowledged authorities on British imperial policy. He was the first Beit
Professor of Colonial History at Oxford from 1905 to 1920. A prolific
writer, Egerton published in 1897* A Short History of British Colonial
Policy *that was printed in nine editions. The following chapter from his
widely read study* The Origin and Growth of Greater Britain *(Oxford:
1903), places the first English empire in its mercantilist context and describes the effects of trade restrictions on English colonies in the New
World.*

It has been already pointed out that the motives which prompted
the European nations to enter upon the field of colonization were in
the main two, viz. the desire to win converts for the Church, and the
desire to win wealth for themselves. Unhappily the missionary zeal was

* Reprinted from *The Origin and Growth of Greater Britain* (Oxford: 1903),
pp. 108–21, with omissions.

soon exhausted. When it was found that the unknown lands were peopled, not by civilized communities (as had been the expectation of Columbus) but by savages, weak for the most part in body and in mind, the work of religion was left to the priest; and laymen more and more confined themselves to the material side of the quest. Moreover, when the tide of Turkish aggression had been finally stemmed at Lepanto,[1] and when the Reformation had opened a fissure in Christendom, the situation became radically altered. Colonists of the Puritan type, it must be admitted, appeared to found their ideal far more upon the Old Testament than upon the New, and, with a few honourable exceptions, seemed to regard the natives as Perizzites and Jebusites to be overthrown, rather than as brothers to become partakers in the mysteries of Christ. It is to the lasting credit of the Roman Catholic Church, and especially of the Jesuit Society, that it never faltered in the prosecution of its mission, and therefore succeeded in influencing the native tribes, whether in Canada, or in Brazil, or Paraguay, as no other Europeans, with the exception perhaps of the Moravian missionaries, have succeeded in influencing them.

Meanwhile, colonies, as the outcome of discovery, could only be justified as means to wealth. As such, the Spanish and Portuguese possessions seemed to have justified themselves abundantly. To all men gold and silver are the most obvious signs of wealth. The bullion which poured into Spain seemed the sure basis of national prosperity. In order, however, to remain rich, it is not enough to have riches, one must also know how to use them. The whole industry of the Spanish possessions was at first thrown into the channel of mining. To such lengths was this carried that the colonists depended for their food, as well as for manufactured goods, on the mother country. At the beginning of the sixteenth century there appears to have been a sudden development of Spanish agriculture and industry. But this was almost wholly due to the introduction of foreign capital and labour, and reactionary measures, which caused the withdrawal of these, nipped this source of prosperity in the bud. Meanwhile, the colonial demand forced up the price of foodstuffs and manufactures, and the Spaniards, unable to meet even the home, much less the colonial, demand, found themselves undersold in their own markets by foreign producers and manufacturers. So little was trade a subject of solicitude, that, in spite of the jealous character of the Spanish régime, protective tariffs were not imposed except to a very small extent. The one aim and object of Spanish policy was to

[1] In 1571 the Spanish defeated the Turks in a famous naval battle at Lepanto off the coast of Greece. [Editor's note.]

prevent the export of bullion. How successful the Spaniards were in this we may learn from the old writer, Mun,[2] who, about 1628, notes that "gold and silver is so scarce in Spain that they are forced to use base copper money." Of course, as Mun points out, "treasure is obtained by a necessity of commerce." It is impossible to doubt but that it was, in part, the object-lesson afforded by Spain's inability to profit by the riches of her colonies, which prompted the policy which is generally known as the mercantile system. The same Mun, whose contemptuous criticism of Spanish methods has been quoted above, is generally acknowledged to have been the first English exponent of the system. The connexions between economic doctrine and colonial development were so close that it is impossible to omit in a book dealing with the genesis of the English colonies all mention of the mercantile system. In Adam Smith's words, "the title of Mun's book, *England's treasure in* (sic) *foreign trade,* became a fundamental maxim in the political economy, not of England only but of all other commercial countries." The golden rule was to sell more to strangers yearly than we consume of theirs in value. Hence the problem of statesmanship became how to increase exports at the expense of imports. For this purpose it was necessary to look to the manufacturer as the source of wealth, and rigidly to disregard the interests of the consumer. It was from this point of view that the system encountered the hostility of Adam Smith, and it is on this ground that it finds its counterpart in the commercial policy of the United States and of other modern countries.

How close was the connexion between trade policy and colonial expansion may be gathered from the following reflection. The well-known chapters of Adam Smith which deal with colonies, the motives of their establishment, the causes of their prosperity, and their advantages, arise incidentally out of the statement that exportations were encouraged under the mercantile system sometimes "by the establishment of colonies," which procured not only particular privileges, but sometimes a monopoly for the goods and merchants of the country which established them. It is impossible then to enter into the spirit of past colonization unless we can form a clear idea of the economic system, which so long controlled both theory and practice.

What then was the mercantile system? Like other things, it changes its aspect from the point of view from which it is regarded. From the point of view of the convinced free trader it is the great mainstay of monopolies and vested interests, but historically it marked a definite

[2] Thomas Mun (1571–1641): English merchant, economist, and publicist; became a director of East India Company (1615). [Editor's note.]

progress from what had gone before. "The essence of the system," writes the German economist, Schmoller, "lies not in some doctrine of money or of the balance of trade; not in tariff barriers, protection duties, or navigation laws; but in something far greater, viz. in the total transformation of society and its organization, as well as of the State and its institutions, in the replacing of a local and territorial economic policy by that of the national State." To cast the weight of the power of the State into the scales of the balance, so as to protect national trade against foreign competition, seemed the natural policy, and it is doubtful whether such policy was not at the time wise. In order to understand the situation we must remember how recent was the sense of national unity political or economic. The splendid ideal of Dante, the divine temporal power, side by side with the divine spiritual power, represented the best thought of the Middle Ages. In conflict with this ideal there were no highly organized States, but merely the anarchy of warring feudal chiefs, and the jealousies of rival town communities. Even in the British Isles, where, for geographical and other reasons, the sense of national life took early root, the neighbourhood of a hostile Scotland and the Hundred Years' War, with its continental interests, retarded the growth of genuine unity. The work of the seventeenth century was to fight its way up from local to national sentiment. Narrow as may appear the ideals of mercantilism, and unjust as may have been its consequences, it is none the less certain that it grew out of a still narrower system, and that the corporate egoism which it embodied was a distinct advance upon the separate egoisms of mediaeval life. Nevertheless, by giving to *national* interests a restricted meaning, which did not include the interests of the colonies, the system sowed the dragon's teeth of future calamity. Its triumph involved the final abandonment of the view that the colonists were merely Englishmen settled beyond the sea, with all the rights and privileges of other Englishmen. That view had been admirably expressed by an early writer: "A State that intends to draw out a colony for the inhabiting of another country must look to the daughters and the mother with an equal eye, remembering that a colony is a part and member of her own body." Henceforth the colonies were to be regarded as "foreign plantations," and, as was pointed out by Seeley,[3] the idea of possession became confused with the idea of settlement.

[3] Sir John R. Seeley (1834–95): English historian renowned for his popularizing of the British empire; author of *The Expansion of England* (1883) and of controversial works on natural religion. [Editor's note.]

The mercantile system, or Colonial Pact, as with unconscious irony it was called in France, found expression in the following restrictions upon freedom of trade. (1) Goods could only be imported into or exported from the colony in ships belonging to the mother country or to the colony. (2) The export trade of the colony was to a great extent confined to the home market. (3) The goods of the mother country obtained a total or partial monopoly in the colonial market; while (4) in return for this, colonial products received preferential treatment in the mother country. Lastly, (5) the colonies were prohibited from setting on foot manufactories so as to compete with the home industries.

(1) For very many years the endeavour of the English legislature had been to secure the trade of England for English ships. At the same time the frequent recurrence of Acts of Parliament with this object in view suggests that such legislation was not very successful. Moreover under the early colonial charters freedom of trade was generally allowed at least for a term of years. In this state of things the active and enterprising Dutch had secured almost the entire carrying trade between England and the colonies. Owing to an abundance of cheap money and of skilled labour, the Dutch were able to build ships at less cost than the cost at which they could be built in England, and were thus able to carry goods with profit at a lower freight than that charged by the English vessels. Mun relates how he had heard "Italians discourse of the simplicity of Englishmen, that their thoughts and jealousies attend only upon the Spanish and French greatness, never once suspecting but constantly embracing the Netherlanders as our best friends and allies; when, in truth, there is no people in Christendom who do more undermine, hurt, and eclipse us daily in our navigation and trade both at home and abroad." The Navigation Act of 1651 proved that the English had learnt the lesson, and the general opinion of, at least, recent economists has been that these laws did help to secure to England its naval supremacy.

An ordinance of 1650 having already forbidden the ships of any foreign nation from coming to or trading with any of the English colonies in America without first obtaining a licence from the English authorities, under the Act of the following year "for increase of shipping and encouragement of the navigation of this nation," no colonial goods could be imported into England or Ireland or any of the colonies unless the ship in which they were brought was owned by an English or colonial proprietor, and had an English captain and a crew, the majority of whom were English. European goods could not be imported into

England or the colonies except in English bottoms, as explained above, or in such foreign ships "as do truly and properly belong to the people of that country or place, of which the said goods are the growth, production, or manufacture." The insertion of this provision explains the intention of the statute. The Dutch were neither producers nor manufacturers, but mainly confined themselves to carrying other nations' wares. The English had reached the conclusion, in Mr. G. L. Beer's words, that one of two alternatives had become necessary: "war à outrance or the closest possible union was the only solution." Neither at this time nor later did the Dutch encourage the idea of union, so that there only remained war—commercial, when not political. The later statute of Charles II, generally known as the First Navigation Act [1660] in substance re-enacted the same provision, except that the proportion of the crew, which must be English, was fixed at three-fourths.

(2) With regard to restrictions upon the export of colonial products, English regulations compared favourably with those of other countries. The first Navigation Law dealt only with shipping, and when, under the Act of Charles II, it was sought also to benefit the English trader by giving him the command of the colonial products, it was only with regard to certain commodities that the English colonies were confined to the market of the mother country. These "enumerated" commodities consisted of sugar, tobacco, cotton-wool, indigo, ginger, fustic or other dyeing material. At a later date hides and skins were placed among the "enumerated" articles, while sugar was in 1731 removed from the list. When in 1705 premiums were granted on the importation of naval stores, including masts, yards, and bowsprits, naval stores were also included among the "enumerated" commodities. The non-enumerated articles could, for very many years, be exported to all parts of the world. When, however, lumber and rice were removed from the list of "enumerated" commodities, their export was confined to countries south of Cape Finisterre, and in the time of George III this provision was extended to all non-enumerated articles. It must be noted that among the non-enumerated articles were some of the most important products of America and the West Indies, e.g. grain of all sorts, salt provisions, and fish. Moreover, there was complete freedom in the intercolonial trade.

With regard to (3) the importation into the colonies of European goods, English policy was, on the whole, generous. It is true that an Act of Charles II compelled all European goods to be first landed in England before being exported to the colonies, but liberal drawbacks were allowed upon the duties paid upon the re-exportation of the goods to the colonies. These drawbacks were intended indeed to benefit the English trader and not the colonist, but their result to the colonies was none the less favourable. The mother country "might frequently suffer both in her revenue by giving back a great part of the duties which had been paid upon the importation of such goods; and in her manufactures by being undersold in the colony markets, in consequence of the easy terms upon which foreign manufactures could be carried thither by means of those drawbacks." But this was no concern of the colonist, and according to Adam Smith, before the passing of an Act of Parliament in 1763, which put matters on a less indulgent footing, "many different sorts of foreign goods might have been bought cheaper in the plantations than in the mother country, and some may still." Hutchinson, the historian of Massachusetts, affirms that after the imposition of the memorable duty upon tea, "poor people in America drank the same tea in quality at 3s. the lb. which the people in England drank at 6s."

(4) In another direction colonial interests were promoted, avowedly and in good faith. Prohibitive duties were placed upon the importation into England of foreign sugar, tobacco, and pig iron, so as to secure the English market for the produce of the colonies. With the same intention the cultivation of tobacco had been strictly forbidden in England. Moreover, the growth of certain products was encouraged by giving bounties upon their export to England. Of these the most important were those connected with naval stores. The practical monopoly which Scandinavia possessed of the tar, pitch, hemp, and timber needed for the navy was for generations a constant source of irritation and possible danger to England. Among the motives which had prompted the colonization of Virginia, one of the most powerful had been the opportunity thus afforded for the production of naval stores. "The masting and caulking of Gloriana's ships" had been already in the thoughts of sixteenth-century discoverers. Nevertheless, in spite of the solicitude of the Board of Trade, and of attempts to form chartered companies for the importation of stores, not much was achieved in this direction. In the reign of Anne [1702–14] bounties were conferred upon the importation into England of tar, pitch, hemp, masts, yards, and bowsprits. . . .

(5) But if even, when his benefit was intended, the independent American preferred very often to gang his own gait, careless of English bounties, it is obvious how irksome to a high-spirited nation must

have been the legislation which sought to prevent it from developing its native manufactures. It is true, of course, that even to the end of the colonial period the grievance was not a very practical one, inasmuch as, in any case, the cheapness of land and the dearness and scarcity of labour must have stood greatly in the way of the development of manufactures. At the same time there had been some manufacturing on a small scale from very early times. As early as 1640 we hear of the manufacture of linen, wool, and other cloths in New England, and there were also ironworks and leather manufactories. The importance of the colonial hat trade is attested by its calling forth an Act of Parliament for its suppression. The woollen industry was the special favourite of English legislation, and an English statute prohibited the export of wool even from one plantation to another. Virginia, Maryland, and the Carolinas, with their staple products, had little temptation to embark in manufactures. It was in New England and New York, where there was no tobacco nor rice to exchange for English goods, that the scarcity of gold and silver made the temptation strong to set on foot domestic industries. . . . With reference to iron, while encouragement was given to the manufacture of pig and bar iron, an absolute prohibition was imposed upon the erection of steel furnaces and slit mills.

Such then was the mercantile system, so far as it affected the relations of mother country and colony. The system involved the theory that the colony was to be always the producer of the raw material, which the industry of the mother country should work up. By implication it denied the equality of colonial Englishmen with Englishmen at home, and by this means poisoned the wells of common patriotism. That Great Britain suffered more than other nations for her adoption of the system was not due to her greater guilt—in fact no other country had treated her colonies so generously—but rather to the material of which her colonists were composed. Planted in a temperate climate, surrounded by difficulties sufficient to make demands upon character, yet not sufficient to paralyse effort, a new people had been growing into manhood, whose full development was to mean the turning of a fresh page in the records of human history. The mercantile system, at worst, wrought pin-pricks on the sturdy frame of the youthful colonies, but pin-pricks are keenly felt and as keenly resented, while the dull pain of the cramping fetters may be borne resignedly for many years. The particular colonies were of course affected very differently by the mercantile system. The southern colonies, Virginia, Maryland, and the Carolinas, found a ready market for their staple products, and suffered little if at all from the action of the mother country. It was in the New England colonies and in New York that the shoe chiefly pinched. Yet even here the opportunities for evasion were so many, and the British official for the most part so helpless in his contest with the slim colonial trader, that it is impossible to gauge the actual effects of British legislation. Perhaps, in the long run, the worst result of the system was the lowering of the public conscience, which is the inevitable outcome of continuous successful evasion of the law. The difficulties of what is known as the critical period of American history, the period which followed upon the close of the War of Independence, were largely the heritage of a time wherein resentment at bad laws had led to contempt of law in general. In the artificial atmosphere of the mercantile system, quack remedies, such as inconvertible paper-money and land banks, found a monstrous growth. It is for their government having been the direct or indirect cause of these economic sins rather than for any acts of actual political misfeasance that Englishmen, in the study of American history, can never quite put off the white sheet.

The dominant policy of the time was well exemplified by the case of the West Indies. In these every encouragement was given to the cultivation of sugar. A practical monopoly was secured in the home market, and the slave trade, which secured a regular supply of labour for the planters, was the object of special solicitude. The interests of the British manufacturers forbade that the colonies should refine their own sugar, and the industry was, so far as possible, confined to the mother country. In this respect English methods compared unfavourably with French, the French islands possessing successful refineries. Adam Smith notes the change which followed the conquest of Grenada by the English.

. . . .

In looking upon the whole history of the mercantile system, the question cannot but occur whether, if mercantilism was a necessary step in the evolution of the modern nation out of the mediaeval locality, it might not have found the remedy for the evils which it undoubtedly brought about, by a yet wider conception which should merge the separate nation in a wider corporate whole. Just as the nation was an advance upon the town community of the Middle Ages, so the nation itself might have given place to the "grand marine empire" advocated by Pownall.[4] An imperial *Zollverein*, with free interchange of com-

---

[4] Thomas Pownall (1722–1805): English colonial administrator; M.P. (1767–80); author of many studies including *The Administration of the Colonies* (1764). [Editor's note.]

modities and uniform duties against the world without, would have been the fulfilment and not the negation of the mercantilist idea. How far such a state of things would have been desirable, and how it would have worked in practice, are difficult questions, which happily we are not concerned to answer. It is enough to note that at the time of the American Revolution, only one voice was raised in favour of such a solution of the problem, that of Thomas Pownall, who had been Governor of Massachusetts. Pownall received no support for his policy either in England or the colonies. Organized interests in England were still too strong to admit the colonists on a footing of complete equality. The thoughts of the colonists themselves had been turned to sterner ways of enforcing their claim to equal rights.

THE FALL OF THE FIRST BRITISH EMPIRE *

Klaus E. Knorr

Professor Klaus E. Knorr is now Director of the Center of International Studies at Princeton University. From his early concern with imperial attitudes in Great Britain he has turned to the study of such issues as American strategic security, foreign economic policy, and scientific capabilities. His book, British Colonial Theories, 1570–1850 *(Toronto: 1944), from which the following excerpts have been taken, provides a comprehensive account of the diverse ideas about colonies that were entertained in England during a span of almost three centuries. The wide gap between theoretical and practical aspects of imperial rule emerges clearly from this study of the protracted debate between the advocates and the opponents of empire.*

In the preceding chapters [of this book] British theories, attitudes, and sentiments in relation to the usefulness of colonial possessions have been presented, roughly, up to the outbreak of the American War of Independence. Conventional and unconventional mercantilist theorizing, the new conceptions of the first classical economists, early projects

---

* Reprinted from *British Colonial Theories, 1570–1850* (Toronto: 1944, 1963), pp. 201–13, with omissions, by permission of the author and the University of Toronto Press. Copyright, 1944, by the University of Toronto.

of imperial federation, and the ideas of the English Dissenters were recorded. All these different currents of opinion were represented in the stream of public comment that accompanied the events of the war. However, the years from 1776 to 1783 were, of course, not conducive to judicious discussion of the problems of empire.

There were gloomy pessimists like the Earl of Shelburne [1] who assumed that "the moment that the independence of America is agreed to by our government, the sun of Great Britain is set, and we shall no longer be a powerful or respectable people." Then there were a few resolute anti-imperialists like Dean Tucker.[2] A group of appeasers propagated a policy of conciliation; this school was composed of men like Chatham [3] and Burke, the Dissenters and large numbers of merchants. The dreadful spectre of war naturally led to further proposals for a federative empire or an imperial union. But the bulk of influential groups were, of course, in favour of forcing the rebellious colonists into subordination to the metropolis. The large majority of the Tories, the King and his friends, the Established Church, and the Armed Services did, on the whole, adhere to this attitude. This was quite natural since the majority opinion was still fully convinced of the utility of the colonies and of the virtues of the Old Colonial System. Moreover, in its strictly legal aspects the British case was strong and the metropolitan demand for a colonial contribution to the expense of governing and defending the Empire was just. Their case had just one defect: it was inexpedient and the attempt to enforce its principles by an appeal to armed force was unwise and futile.

Before the war in America looked entirely hopeless from the English standpoint, proposals were brought forward which contemplated the possibility of saving at least part of the North American Empire in addition to Canada. William Knox,[4] for example, approached the Gov-

---

[1] 2d Earl of Shelburne and 1st Marquess of Lansdowne (1737–1805): Secretary of State (1766–68); First Lord of Treasury and Prime Minister (1782–83); favored conciliation of American colonies. [Editor's note.]

[2] Josiah Tucker (1712–99): English economist and dean of Gloucester; wrote many tracts on economic, colonial, and religious subjects; opposed mercantilist policies. [Editor's note.]

[3] William Pitt, Earl of Chatham (1708–78): English statesman who guided the country's fortunes during the Seven Years' War until his resignation (1761); opponent of harsh policies toward the colonies; formed another ministry (1766–68), despite poor health; father of the "Younger Pitt" who became Prime Minister (1783–1801, 1804–05). [Editor's note.]

[4] (1732–1810): colonial official; joint undersecretary for the Colonies (1770–82); author of numerous pamphlets on colonial and other public affairs. [Editor's note.]

ernment with a plan that envisaged, somewhat immediately, "the establishment of a port on the Chesapeak, and . . . expeditions for the recovery of Georgia and South Carolina; . . . the retaining them, with the islands of New York, Statin, Long Island, Canada, and Nova Scotia, would . . . secure to this country all the trade of America which was worth having, at a much less charge to the Nation, than we had hitherto been at for that country."

Shortly before the end of the war, Sir John Sinclair [5] wrote a pamphlet which suggested several alternatives to the "total" abandonment of the North American colonies. One of them contemplated the retention of "some posts on the continent." Charleston, he thought, might be rendered impregnable against the American armies. It would "insure to us some of the most lucrative branches of the American trade" and, besides, would serve as an "asylum" for "the unfortunate loyalists." As another alternative Sinclair suggested the abandonment of the North American continent followed by a determined attack on the French West Indies. These colonies would not be able

to resist the efforts of a spirited attack; and, heavy as the charges of the war have been, there is every reason to believe that we could conquer possessions from that nation, whose value would nearly repay the expences we have been put to: or, if France is thought to be an enemy whose colonies cannot easily be mastered, we are likely to find the continental possessions of Spain a very easy acquisition. . . . The possession of almost any province in that part of the world, would enable us to acquire the greatest part of the trade of Spanish America, and would amply compensate for the treasure we have lost.

These various proposals, however, by no means exhausted the inventive imagination of Sir John Sinclair. He offered a final alternative proposing as a convenient sequel to the disruption of the British Empire, the general emancipation of European colonies in America.

Yet the course of events that forced the British to accept defeat, destroyed whatever hopes there might have been of retaining, besides Canada, a portion of the American continental empire. Instead of hopes there was defeatism and resignation. Not a few, some sincerely and some in a rather forced manner—the grapes had turned sour—, expressed their acceptance of the loss. Thus, the Earl of Stair,[6] "the Cassandra of

---

[5] (1754–1835): financier and noted agriculturist: M.P. (1780–1811); first president of Board of Agriculture (1793–98, 1806–13). [Editor's note.]

[6] John Dalrymple, 5th Earl of Stair (1720–89): Scottish peer who advocated conciliating the American colonies and wrote on such questions as national finance. [Editor's note.]

the State," ever mindful of the need for strictest economy and horrified at mounting public debts, said: "Having profited so little by our foreign Excursions, let us turn Homewards, and try what Precedent and Experience will do for us there."

A review of the typical arguments used by those who perceived advantages in what appeared an irreparable loss to the majority of the the nation, reveals some interesting points. First, it was agreed among this school of thought that the subject of the utility of colonies required much more analytical effort than had been bestowed upon it hitherto. James Anderson [7] declared: "It has appeared to me not a little extraordinary, that among the many treatises which have been written of late, in consequence of the dispute between Great Britain and her colonies, no attempt should have been made to ascertain with some degree of precision wherein consist the advantages that have accrued to the mother country, or the disadvantages that may be expected to be felt by her in consequence of her connection with the American colonies."

While the supposed profitability of the metropolitan monopoly of the colony trade had formed the centre of mercantilist reasoning on the usefulness of colonies and the *raison d'être* of the Old Colonial System, the writers here considered, viewed the loss of this monopoly from two different standpoints. The reaction of one group was influenced by conceptions which belittled the importance and utility of any trade carried on beyond the national frontiers and advised concentration on agriculture and the cultivation of the home market. Other writers, on the other hand, came to the conclusion, soon to be substantiated by experience, that the loss of the colonies would not materially diminish the flow of this trade. The Earl of Stair remarked: "Whenever the war ceases, it is highly probable that much of the antient Intercourse betwixt this Country and her American Brethren will be renewed, perhaps on a Footing not much less advantageous than formerly. . . ."

Henceforth the fact, realized by a great many people, that Great Britain had been able to keep a large share of American foreign trade, that the mother country had lost nothing "except the barren honour of sovereignty," was exploited both by the critics of the Old Colonial System and by the anti-imperialists. The same experience, however, furnished the basis for a stock-argument with those expansionist imperialists who had discarded the out-worn principles underlying the monopolist system. Later they were to point out that there are "invisible and more pleasing ties of similar habits, laws, and, above all, language,"

[7] (1739–1808): Scottish agriculturist and economist who anticipated David Ricardo's theory of rent. [Editor's note.]

which produce a natural "monopoly" bare of any kind of metropolitan "compulsion."

Many writers acknowledged that the emancipation of the Northern American colonies had relieved the United Kingdom of a considerable financial burden. Macpherson,[8] for example, affirmed that "relief from the expense of governing and protecting them" was one of the beneficial consequences of American independence. "Among the lesser advantages may be reckoned the relief from the payment of bounties, which had been very liberally granted for the encouragement of many articles of American cultivation, that can now be imported without taxing the people of this country for the benefit of the American planters." Chalmers [9] likewise concluded that "while this nation has saved the annual expense of great military and civil establishments, it can hardly be said to have lost any commercial profits." He also pointed out that Great Britain had gained in power by the emancipation of the colonies.

I have long thought, what I now think, that those colonies, from the peace of 1763 to the epoch of their revolt, formed balances to the power, rather than buttresses to the strength of Great Britain. Experience has evinced, what Tucker had taught, that we should derive, from the independence of those colonies, all the advantages of their trade, without the vexations, and weaknesses, of their government. . . . If it be true, then, that our resources, and strength, lie in the People of the United Kingdom, what do we lose, by the several relinquishments of the Preliminary Treaty? Do we lose men? No. Do we lose money? No. Would they have been expensive establishments, during peace? Yes. Would they have been a still greater source of weakness, in war? Yes.

One advantage which some writers attributed to American independence was seen in connection with the monopoly enjoyed by British shipping. It is remarkable that the same authors who applauded the loss of the monopoly of the colony trade, saw a gain in the fact that American shipping could now be excluded from Britain's imperial trade. Consideration of English maritime power was, of course, the reason for this attitude. Macpherson stated: ". . . a very important advantage was the recovery of the valuable trade of ship-building, which had in great measure been, very impolitically, sacrificed to the zeal for

[8] James Macpherson (1736–96): controversial Scottish poet, translator, and historian; M.P. (1780–96); wrote political tracts for government after 1766. [Editor's note.]
[9] George Chalmers (1742–1825): Scottish antiquarian and publicist; chief clerk of committee of privy council for trade and foreign plantations (1786); author of many works on politics, literature, and empire. [Editor's note.]

promoting the prosperity of the colonies, insomuch that, notwithstanding the very great inferiority of the greatest part of the American oak, a large portion of the vessels belonging to the different ports of Great Britain were built in America." Chalmers concluded that the loss of the colonies had conferred "a real advantage" on Great Britain. "It is, indeed, fortunate for us, that the French were so much blinded, by the splendour of giving independence to the British colonies, as not to see distinctly how much their interposition and their aid promoted the real advantage of Great Britain. . . . And they have even conferred on the people, whom they wished to depress, actual strength, by restoring, unconsciously, the ship-building, the freights, and the fisheries; of which the colonists had too much partaken. . . ."

As for that part of the Empire which was left intact in 1783, some observers regretted that the Canadas had not been relinquished too. John Nicholls,[10] for example, held that it would be very difficult to defend these provinces against the United States, that Upper Canada was likely to desire incorporation into the Union and that Lower Canada was without value to Britain. "What have we not already expended on these provinces? and if they are to be defended, what sum is not probable that we shall waste before we get rid of them?"

. . . .

The foregoing review of a sample of British reactions to the emancipation of the American colonies poses these important questions: to what extent did these views represent metropolitan opinion as a whole? What was the general trend of British thought after the independence of the United States had become an irrevocable fact and the first British Empire had collapsed in a most spectacular fashion?

There is no ready and unambiguous answer to these questions. The Empire had been disrupted beyond apparent prospect of repair and the very process of its disruption had occasioned formidable losses in men, money, and prestige. All the mercantilist arguments, supposedly showing the utility of colonies under the Old Colonial System, had been theoretically exploded. Novel doctrines of foreign trade and of economic activity in general had introduced new conceptions that were bound to influence any serious consideration of the value of colonial dependencies whether under a closed or a free trade system.

In view of these facts the relatively small number of those who ad-

[10] (1746?–1832): M.P. (1783–87, 1796–1802); author of *Recollections and Reflections*. [Editor's note.]

vocated an anti-imperialist programme is amazing. It may be true that
the English people "fell into a kind of disgust with colonial matters"
and that the nation was filled with "confusion" and "lethargy" as regards colonial affairs. Yet mingled with disgust and confusion was the
dogged determination to hold fast to the possession and exploitation of
the remnants of the Old Empire. For a long time to come, this attitude
had, at bottom, little to do with the contents of different colonial theories. It was not susceptible to intellectual arguments. Indeed, the colonial theories brought forward by the classical economists and the
Philosophical Radicals were never refuted on an intellectually credit-
able level of reasoning. No matter how often and how brilliantly the
out-worn arguments of the mercantilists were disproved, they were
advanced again and again with tedious monotony. Any study of influential opinion on the colonial question during the half-century following the defection of the United States requires frequent indication of the
relative weight which the various arguments carried with the general
public.

Before 1783, the opinions of the intellectual leaders of public opinion were, on the whole, in line with that of the bulk of influential
groups. After 1783 a situation arose in which the intellectual *élite* of
Great Britain, eminently articulate on the colonial question, was opposed by the broad mass of influential groups which were rather inartic-
ulate and chary of expressing reasoned opinions on the subject. Nevertheless this majority seemed to know exactly what they wanted and
were apparently unperturbed by the argumentative "broadsides" of their
intellectually superior opponents. This fact is clearly revealed by a
perusal of parliamentary records. Quantitatively the speeches delivered
by the contending groups appear about evenly balanced; qualitatively,
the arguments of the minority seem, to the objective observer, far superior to those advanced by the majority. But, almost invariably, what
really mattered was the list of division.

It is by no means difficult to account for the conditions that brought
about this situation. Public opinion, on any matter and at any time, is
determined by an incredibly confused maze of thoughts and sentiments, prejudices and traditions, more or less closely related to the
supposed interests of the specific carrier of opinion. To disentangle,
weigh, and label these various constituent elements with precision in
any concrete case defies the analytical tools at the disposal of the observer. Yet, in the special case here under consideration, the following
rough conclusions may be hazarded without too much risk: In the

spheres of traditionalism and of national pride of empire the attachment of large influential groups to the symbols of empire remained impervious to intellectual arguments. Large sections, no doubt, were prevented from grasping these arguments because they were intellectually too lazy, incapable, or unschooled. Most important, however, was that a great many interest-groups, who had a selfish stake in the preservation of the old system, wielded a disproportionate influence in politics.

It is certain that the American War of Independence did not lead to any widespread indifference toward the remainder of the Empire. Indeed, it may be said that the fall of the first Empire was accompanied by the birth of the second. When following Cornwallis's surrender at Yorktown, in April, 1782, Rodney defeated the French fleet in the Battle of the Saints, the British recovered their undisputed command of the seas and made the establishment of the second Empire not only possible but, in view of the attitude of the English ruling groups, almost inevitable. Immediately after the Peace of Paris the centre of imperial interest shifted to Canada in the West and to India in the East.

That the revolt of the American colonists taught the imperial ruling groups in England a lesson in how to govern colonies wisely is nothing but a legend. Constitutionally and politically, imperial rule was not relaxed but tightened. The rebellious Americans, as has been pointed out, had enjoyed a great deal of freedom in political respect. Hence, when these colonies revolted while Canada remained loyal, it seemed to the majority of the metropolitan ruling group that this large amount of political freedom had fostered a spirit of democracy and independence which, in turn, had caused the revolution. It was for this reason that the government, determined to keep what was left of the Empire, now embarked upon a reactionary course and imposed upon its old and new colonies a system of centralized supervision and control that was to be maintained for more than half a century.

On the other hand, in regard to economic colonial policies, the former system of mutual preferences and monopolies was retained to be sure, but soon this arrangement began to operate almost entirely in favour of the colonies (excepting the West Indies). This was the result, not only of new preferences granted to the colonies, but also of the increase of Britain's capacity to produce manufactures more cheaply than her European rivals and of her growing capacity to consume colonial articles. Thus, while during the ante-revolution period the imperial régime had been restrictive of the economic development of the colonies but rather liberal in the sphere of politics, this situation was . . . almost reversed after 1783: the colonies were to exploit the mother country commercially while the latter ruled her dependencies in a stern and, sometimes, despotic fashion.

What led, in the final analysis, to a gradual liberalization of the political imperial régime, to the abolition of the system of imperial monopolies and preferences, and even to a widespread indifference toward the colonies, was not the experience of the American War of Independence but the effect of the rapid progress of the Industrial Revolution in England.

THE NEW IMPERIALISM: THE HOBSON– LENIN THESIS REVISED *

D. K. Fieldhouse

David K. Fieldhouse, author of this lucid analysis of the historiography of British imperialism, is Beit Lecturer in the History of the British Commonwealth at Oxford University. His examination of the Hobsonian interpretation of the new imperialism provides a useful summary of the issues involved in the controversy over the origins of British imperial expansion. He finds that what was new about the "new" imperialism (that is, imperialism after 1870) is not an economic but a political phenomenon. In pointing up the fallacies of Hobson's explanation of the race for colonies after 1870, Fieldhouse leans heavily on the Gallagher-Robinson distinction between formal and informal empire, which is discussed later in this volume.

It is now nearly sixty years since J. A. Hobson published *Imperialism: a Study* [1902], and thereby gave the word the connotation it still generally carries. His conception of the nature of "imperialism" [1] has, indeed, been almost universally accepted and, partly through the expository literature it has generated, may be said to have exercised a

---

* Reprinted from "'Imperialism': An Historiographical Revision," *The Economic History Review*, 2d Series, XIV, No. 2 (1961), 187–209, with omissions, by permission of the author and the Economic History Society.

[1] When used in Hobson's sense, the word will here be printed in quotation marks. [Editor's note.]

significant historical influence. Yet, for all its success, Hobson's argument has always been extremely vulnerable to criticism: and it is therefore surprising that those historians and economists who have argued effectively that his analysis is basically unsound should have received so little attention. The aim of the present article is to draw together some of the more important arguments that have been put forward for and against his thesis, and to suggest that, on balance, the noes have it.

Hobson's own claim to importance and originality lies simply in his having induced British, and subsequently world, opinion to accept his own special definition of the word imperialism. Professor Koebner has already examined the various meanings given to the word before 1902.[2] He has suggested that, as used in England, it had two general connotations in the 1890's, both of which were morally neutral. In one sense, it was being used of those who wished to prevent the existing British settlement colonies from seceding and becoming independent states, and was therefore a conservative factor. In another, and increasingly common, sense, it was being used to indicate an expansionist and "forward" attitude towards problems connected with the future control of the "uncivilized" parts of the world, such as Africa, the Middle East and the Pacific. Salisbury was, in this sense, regarded as an imperialist in accepting the need for Britain to share in the partition of East Africa. Gladstone, in opposing the acquisition of Uganda, was emphatically anti-imperialist, even though he had acquiesced in the need to gain some control over Egypt in 1882.[3] In the eyes of the anti-imperialists the sin of expansionism lay in the waste of money it entailed on armaments, in the cost of colonial governments, and in the danger of international conflicts over intrinsically unimportant territories which it would be wiser to leave alone. As a rule no worse motive was attributed to the imperialists than "jingoism" or excessive concern with Britain's position as a great power.

But, between 1896 and 1902, imperialism, as a word, began to lose its innocence. Koebner has shown that events in South Africa, and particularly the Jameson Raid, gave rise to a suspicion that, here at

---

[2] See note 1 page 2 above. [Editor's note.]

[3] 3rd Marquess of Salisbury (1830–1903): Conservative party leader and Prime Minister (1885–86, 1886–92, 1895–1902); also Foreign Secretary (1878–80, 1885–86, 1887–92, 1895–1900). Throughout most of his career Lord Salisbury was a fervent opponent of William Ewart Gladstone (1809–98): leader and principal inspiration of the Liberal party; Prime Minister (1868–74, 1880–85, 1886, 1892–94); Member of Parliament for over sixty years. [Editor's note.]

least, the expansive urge was motivated by something other than a concern for national greatness, by what Harcourt called "stock-jobbing imperialism"—based on the interests of financiers. This was, of course, a special case; and a distinction remained between an honest, even if misguided, imperialism, and the debased variety to be seen on the Rand. Yet the idea now gained ground that South Africa might not, after all, be a special case, but might exhibit in an extreme form a factor inherent in all expansionism. By 1900 radical opinion had moved so far in this direction that the Fifth International Socialist Congress, taught probably by its English delegation, could resolve

. . . que le développement du capitalisme mène fatalement à l'expansion coloniale . . .: que la politique coloniale de la bourgeoisie n'a d'autre but que d'élargir les profits de la classe capitaliste et le maintien du système capitaliste . . .[4]

Here, in a nutshell, was Hobson's doctrine of "imperialism." But it remained to be seen whether such a dogmatic interpretation would ever command a wide support: and it was essentially his achievement to ensure that, in his own non-Marxist form, it should become the generally accepted theory.

Hobson's *Imperialism* therefore came out at a time when British public opinion, disillusioned by the Boer war, was already profoundly suspicious about the motives behind recent imperial expansion. It was, in fact, a pamphlet for the times, rather than a serious study of the subject; and, like all pamphlets that achieve influence, it owed much of its success to the fact that it expressed a current idea with peculiar clarity, force and conviction. It arose immediately out of Hobson's visit to South Africa during the war, and derived from reports he sent back to *The Speaker*, which were published as a book in 1900 as *The War in South Africa, Its Causes and Effects*. Yet, paradoxically, Hobson was not primarily concerned with imperial problems: and *Imperialism* can only be properly understood on the basis that his interest, then and throughout his life, was with the social and economic problems of Britain. In a sense, this book was primarily a vehicle for publicizing the theory of "underconsumption," which he regarded as his main intellectual achievement, and which he expressed more fully in *The Evolution of Modern Capitalism*, and other works. In

[4] "that the development of capitalism leads inevitably to colonial expansion . . . that the colonial policy of the bourgeoisie has no other aim than the increase of profits for the capitalist class and the maintenance of the capitalist system . . ." [Editor's note.]

brief, the theory, which was an alternative to the Marxist concept of surplus value as an explanation of poverty, saw excessive investment by the capitalist, with its concomitant of underconsumption by the wage-earner, as the root cause of recurrent slumps, of low interest rates, and of permanent under-employment. Hobson thought there were only two answers to this problem. The correct one—which would also be the answer to the "condition of England question"—was to increase the buying power of the workers by giving them a higher share of the profits of industry. The wrong one, which was no answer to the social question, was to invest the surplus capital overseas, where it could earn a high interest rate, and thus sustain domestic rates of interest, without benefiting the British worker. And this, he held, was what Britain had been doing since at least the middle of the nineteenth century.

To this point the economic theory, though highly vulnerable, has no apparent relevance to the phenomenon of overseas expansion, that is, to imperialism. The key to Hobson's theory of "imperialism" lies in the connexion he makes between the two.

Overproduction in the sense of an excessive manufacturing plant, and surplus capital which could not find sound investments within the country, forced Great Britain, Germany, Holland, France to place larger and larger portions of their economic resources outside the area of their present political domain, and then stimulate a policy of political expansion so as to take in the new areas.

Thus "imperialism," in the special sense used by Hobson, is an external symptom of a social malady in the metropolitan countries. Without this domestic pressure for investment overseas, there would be no effective impulse towards the acquisition of new colonies. Conversely, without colonies, capital would lack an outlet, and domestic rates of interest would sink . . .

It is not proposed at this stage to examine Hobson's theory in detail: but some comment must be made on the logical value of the argument he uses to demonstrate the historical truth of this hypothesis. Does he, in fact, supply any evidence to support the claim that colonies were the product of a demand either for new investment opportunities, or for security for existing investments? He begins with a straightforward account of the expansion of the European empires since 1870, printing a list of territories acquired by Britain. Then, in chapter two, he demonstrates that the expansion of the British empire had been of little apparent value to British trade; that trade with these recent acquisitions was the least valuable part of intra-imperial trade; and that British trade with all colonies was declining in relation to trade with the rest of the world. Clearly, then, "imperialism" was not good for trade. Nor was it good for emigration (which, in any case, he thought unnecessary), since these new tropical colonies were quite unsuited to white settlement. And his conclusion was that

The Imperialism of the last six decades is clearly condemned as a business policy, in that at enormous expense it has procured a small, bad, unsafe increase of markets, and has jeopardised the entire wealth of the nation in arousing the strong resentment of other nations . . .

How then can a motive be found for this imperial expansion? The motive is to be seen if, alongside the list of territorial acquisitions, is placed a table showing the increase of British overseas investments in the same period. It then becomes obvious that, during the period in which British possessions had increased by 4,754 m. square miles and by a population of 88 millions, British overseas investments had also increased enormously—from £144 m. to £1698 m. between 1862 and 1893 alone. Could there be any doubt that the two sets of figures were intimately connected as cause and effect? Hobson had no doubts about it: "It is not too much to say that the modern foreign policy of Great Britain has been primarily a struggle for profitable markets of investment."

But it is immediately apparent that Hobson had in no sense proved that there was any connexion between the investments made overseas and the territory acquired contemporaneously. His table of investments makes no differentiation between the areas in which investment had taken place, beyond such classifications as "Foreign," "Colonial," "U.S.A." and "Various," and, in fact, he assumes quite arbitrarily that the new colonies had attracted a high proportion of the investment called "Foreign" (i.e. before they were annexed) or "Colonial" (subsequent to annexation). This, it will be suggested below, is a basic fault of his theory of "imperialism." Indeed, to put the case bluntly, Hobson performed an intellectual conjuring trick. Convinced of the essential truth of his economic theory, he deceived the eye by the speed of his hand, creating the illusion that, of the two sets of statistics he held up, one was the cause of the other.

It is not possible here to consider the rest of Hobson's *Imperialism*, interesting though it is in relation to related controversies over protection, tariff reform and imperial unity. But two additional points in his main argument must be mentioned because they were intrinsic to his definition of the origins and nature of "imperialist" expansion.

The first of these concerns the relationship between the financial interest and other "imperialists," and is therefore crucial to his theory. He was aware that, contrary to his argument, the obvious driving force of British expansion since 1870 appeared to lie in the explorers, missionaries, engineers, patriotic pressure groups, and empire-minded politicians, all of whom had evident influence, and had demonstrable interests, other than those of investment, in territorial acquisitions. And he was equally aware that if the impulse to expansion could be satisfactorily explained in the old-fashioned terms of their idealism, their ambition, or their concern with the status of Britain as a world power, rather than in terms of the self-interest of the capitalist, his own central thesis would collapse. It was therefore necessary that these men . . . should be shown to be mere puppets—the tools of "imperialism" rather than its authors. Hobson did this by falling back on what may be called the "faceless men" gambit:

Finance manipulates the patriotic forces which politicians, soldiers, philanthropists, and traders generate; the enthusiasm for expansion which issues from these sources, though strong and genuine, is irregular and blind; the financial interest has those qualities of concentration and clear-sighted calculation which are needed to set Imperialism to work. An ambitious statesman, a frontier soldier, an overzealous missionary, a pushing trader, may suggest or even initiate a step of imperial expansion, may assist in educating patriotic public opinion to the urgent need of some fresh advance, but the final determination rests with the financial power.

In this ingenious way Hobson inverted the apparent relationship between the obvious "imperialists" and the investor. Instead of the financier being induced to invest in new possessions, with more or less enthusiasm, once political control had been imposed for other reasons, he becomes the essential influence in the take-over itself. Investment no longer follows the flag: it decides where it is profitable to plant it, and tells the government whether it is to follow the advice of men of action or of ideas in each particular case. Thus, "imperialism" can never be interpreted as the spontaneous expression of the idealism, the chauvinism or the mere energy of a nation. In its practical form it is the expression of the special interests of the financier behind the scenes, who decides whether it is worth his while to allow a dream to become a reality, and who alone will reap the benefits. . . .

The other essential point in the theory of "imperialism" is the suggestion that the possession of colonies by individual capitalist states results automatically in the exploitation of the indigenous peoples of Africa and Asia. In his long chapter "Imperialism and the Lower Races," which is in many ways one of the most undogmatic and constructive parts of the book, Hobson argued that exploitation, whether by appropriation of land, or by the use of cheap labour—forced or nominally free—in mines, farms and factories, had been a general feature of the colonies of all the European powers. Hobson, in the British humanitarian tradition, thought such exploitation to be both wrong and inexpedient. Economic development was good for undeveloped colonies and for the world as a whole. The danger lay in allowing the financiers to use the political power of the imperial authority for their own purposes; and the solution was for international control of colonies—the germ of the later mandate concept—and patience in allowing normal economic forces to give the natives an inducement to work freely in European enterprises. Sensible as his general attitude was, it is clear that Hobson had thus included in "imperialism" the suggestion that countries possessing colonies were almost certain to exploit them in their own interests; and this argument was to become a staple of later critics of "colonialism."

II

The theory of "imperialism" as it developed after the publication of Hobson's *Study* continued to be founded on the three main concepts outlined above. Yet, in examining its historiography, it is clear that it was Lenin, writing in 1916, rather than Hobson himself, who gave "imperialism" its dogmatic coherence and much of its eventual influence. It is therefore necessary to consider briefly the extent to which Lenin [in his *Imperialism, the Highest Stage of Capitalism*, 1916] modified Hobson's ideas.

The greatest difference lies in the first and most important part of the argument; that is, in the nature of the internal pressure in the capitalist countries which forces them to expand their colonial possessions. Hobson had explained this pressure in terms of "under-consumption": but Lenin naturally had a more orthodox theory to hand. Capitalism as a system was approaching the apocalypse Marx had foretold. Competitive capitalism had, in the late nineteenth century, been replaced by "monopoly capitalism," with its characteristic agencies, the cartels, trusts and tariffs. It was no longer dynamic, but anxious only to maintain its profit margins by more intensive exploitation of limited and protected markets. Moreover, the "finance-capitalists"—the banks and trusts—who now largely controlled capital itself, found that, under monopoly conditions, it was more profitable to employ surplus capital abroad than in domestic industry. At home, it could only increase production, lower prices, and raise wages. Abroad it could give a high interest return without any of these consequences. But, to gain the highest return from overseas investment it was desirable to have some political control over the territory in which the investment was made. This might be in the limited form of a "semi-colony," such as the Argentine. But only in the colony proper could really comprehensive economic and political controls be imposed which would give investments their highest return. The result had been the competition between the great powers to acquire new colonies after 1870, which would continue until the whole uncivilized world had come under imperial rule. Then would follow the inter-imperial wars for the redivision of the empires, leading to proletarian revolutions in the "imperialist" states, the creation of "socialist" states, and so, automatically, to the end of "imperialism."

How much, then, does Lenin's explanation of the force behind "imperialism" differ from that of Hobson? Fundamentally, only in this: that, whereas Hobson used his theory as evidence that social-democratic reform at home was necessary and possible to eliminate the evil of "under-consumption" and therefore make "imperialism" unnecessary, Lenin made "imperialism" the definition of an inherent and unavoidable stage in the growth of capitalist society which could not be "reformed." Hobson was a doctor prescribing a remedy, Lenin a prophet forecasting catastrophe. But, while they disagreed as to the precise causes, both maintained that there existed in the "capitalist" countries a tremendous pressure for overseas investment, and that this was the main factor in producing "imperialist" expansion after 1870.

On Hobson's second point—the control and influence exercised by "finance" over government and over the men who actually carved out the new empires—there is little difference between them. Lenin, if anything, went further, ignoring the theory that in a democratic country like Britain Hobson's "imperialists" found it necessary to corrupt public opinion through the press; and assuming, on the basis of Marxist theory and German experience, that the financial power of the banks and trusts was now so great that governments virtually did

as they were told by the "finance-capitalist." . . . There is no room
here for explaining the actions of governments in any terms other
than of the economics of "imperialism."

On Hobson's third point, Lenin had little explicit to say. As a
Marxist he assumed it to be axiomatic that all workers were exploited
by capital; so that a colony would differ from the metropolis only in
the fact that the exploiting capitalist was an alien, and colonies merely
added to the pool of labour from which he could extract "surplus
value."

With the publication of Lenin's book it may be said that the concept of "imperialism" had reached its mature form; for, on points on
which they differed, Lenin's interpretation has generally been the
dominant one. The subsequent historiography of the subject on the
"imperialist" side of the argument has tended to fall into two main
categories—either glosses on the theory, or applications of it to the
actual events of the period after 1870.

.   .   .   .

III

The central feature of the theory of "imperialism," by which it
must stand or fall, is the assertion that the empires built up after 1870
were not an option but a necessity for the economically advanced
states of Europe and America: that these capitalist societies, because
of their surplus of domestically produced capital, were forced to export
capital to the under-developed regions of the world: and that it was
only this investment—prospective or existing—that supplied a motive
for the acquisition of new colonies.

Faced with this theory, the historian who does not take its truth
for granted is likely to be sceptical on at least three main grounds.
First, his instinct is to distrust all-embracing historical formulas which,
like the concept of "the rise of the middle class," seek to explain
complex developments in terms of a single dominant influence. Again,
he is likely to suspect an argument that isolates the imperial expansion
of the period after 1870 from all earlier imperial developments if only
because he is aware of so many elements of continuity in the history
of overseas empires over the past few centuries. But, above all, he must
be aware that the theory simply does not appear to fit the facts of the
post-1870 period as he knows them. Looking, for example, at Hobson's

list of territories acquired by Britain after 1870, it seems, at first sight at least, difficult to believe that any considerable part of them were annexed either because British capitalists had already invested much of their surplus capital there, or because they regarded them as fields for essential future investment. In some cases, perhaps, it seems that a *prima facie* case could be made out on these lines—for Egypt, the Transvaal and Rhodesia, to take Hobson's three main examples. But, even in these, further consideration must arouse doubts. Surely the strategic importance of the Suez Canal was as good a reason for controlling Egypt in 1882 as the preservation of the interests of the bond holders in the Canal Company. Was it really necessary, on purely economic grounds, to annex the Transvaal in 1899 when the British mine-owners were making vast fortunes under Kruger's government, and had shown themselves so divided over the question of the Jameson Raid and the independence of the Republic? Again, granted that Rhodes and the British South Africa Company had excellent economic reasons for wanting British control over Rhodesia, was their anxiety really due to the pressure of British funds waiting for investment opportunity?

Doubts such as these concerning even the key examples chosen by Hobson inevitably stimulate further examination of his list: and this makes it clear that not even a *prima facie* case could be made out for most of the territories he includes. To take a random selection, it would surely be ludicrous to suggest that Fiji, British New Guinea or Upper Burma were annexed in order to protect large British investments, or even as a field for subsequent investment. In each case secular explanations seem fully to account for their annexation: the chaotic condition of a mixed society in the Pacific, the fears of Australia for her military security, and the frontier problems of India. And even where, as in Malaya, large capital investment did take place after annexation, the time factor must be considered. Were the British investor and the government really so alert to the possible future need for fields for investment? Or did annexation in fact take place for quite other reasons, being followed by investment when new conditions and new possibilities arose which were then totally unforeseen?

.   .   .   .

It has been seen that this theory of surplus capital being forced out into the undeveloped world was expressed differently by Hobson and Lenin, and it will be convenient to consider Lenin's theory first. This was, it will be remembered, that the centrifugal force in the capitalist countries was the interest of the monopolistic "finance-capitalists" who stood only to lose by investment at home.

In this the fallacy is immediately obvious. If it was true of any country, it was not true of Britain; for no one could maintain that British capital was then controlled by a few trusts or even cartels. These, of course, did exist in Britain, such as the Salt Union of 1888, the United Alkali Company of 1897, and others in textiles, shipping and steel. But, whatever the desires of their founders, they were in fact small, tentative and generally unsuccessful. British capital, whatever its tendencies, was still "competitive" on Lenin's definition: and he in fact admitted that in Britain "monopoly" must be taken to mean the reduction of the competing enterprises to "a couple of dozen or so." This is hardly a satisfactory explanation of the need to export capital on a vast scale; so, presumably, Britain must have other reasons both for this and for territorial annexation. But, for different reasons, other countries also escape from the formula. Germany was Lenin's main example of the country dominated by trusts: but, as Professor Hancock has pointed out, the age of German cartels came only after about 1900, while the main German grab for colonies had taken place during the previous twenty years. And America, which certainly had vast industrial and financial combinations, proved, in spite of Roosevelt's attempt to create an expansionist movement, to be the least "imperialist" of all the capitalist states. It would therefore seem reasonable to conclude that Lenin's narrow explanation for the export of capital and the concurrent extension of European political control overseas is unacceptable.

Yet, whatever reasons are assigned to it, the fact of vast capital exports from the advanced countries in the period after 1870 remains. . . . Hence, the important questions must be faced. Was there in fact a vast reservoir of capital, generated (for example) in Britain, which was available for overseas investment? Why was it invested abroad rather than at home? And was it in fact invested in those areas which were annexed as colonies after 1871?

The publication in 1953 of Professor A. K. Cairncross's *Home and Foreign Investment 1870–1913* has made it possible to approach these questions from a new and non-doctrinaire angle. The key to his interpretation lay in his rejection of Hobson's naive model of the British capitalist, embarrassed by an excess of capital, which could not be invested at home because of the "under-consumption" factor, sending it abroad into undeveloped tropical territories where it would produce a high rate of interest. Instead, it is necessary to see that capital exports were not divorced from the economy of Great Britain but were in fact a necessary concomitant of the pattern of British trade and development. It can be shown that in fact the great majority of this capital went to the "new" countries—to the United States, Canada, Argentine, Australasia and South Africa in particular—who were producing the primary materials that the British economy needed, and who had to have capital to expand their production for British consumption. To invest in these countries was therefore, in one sense, to invest in a primary sector of the British economy itself. And the return to Britain was not entirely, or even primarily, in a tribute of money, but in cheap and plentiful raw materials and food.

Moreover, far from weakening the British economy and reducing the living standards of the working class as both Hobson and Lenin thought they did, these capital exports were essential to both. Indeed, Cairncross argued convincingly that, by creating a demand for British products, these investments simultaneously kept up the level of profits at home, kept down the level of unemployment, and maintained wage levels. And, as the rate of overseas investment seems to have been greatest when the terms of trade were against Britain—the 1880's being an exceptional period when special factors in the United States offset the general tendency—Cairncross concludes that "it was foreign investment that pulled Britain out of most depressions before 1914." . . . In fact it can be said that the British investor did not choose to invest abroad simply to get high interest rates, but, by and large, to get a slightly higher rate than on an equivalent type of stock at home. Above all, if he chose to invest in a British colony, it was not because he expected higher interest, but because he wanted greater security than he would get in an equivalent foreign investment. If he wanted a "risk" investment—diamonds, copper, gold, nitrates, etc.—he went for it wherever the enterprise happened to be situated. But, in proportion to the whole, investments of this type were very small in 1911.

But, for the present argument, the third and most important fact that emerges . . . is that Hobson was entirely wrong in assuming that any large proportion of British overseas investment went to those undeveloped parts of Africa and Asia which were annexed during the "imperialist" grab after 1870. As Professor Nurkse has remarked of Hobson:

Had he tried to do what he did for trade, that is, to show the geographical distribution of overseas investment, he would have found that British capital tended to bypass the primitive tropical economies and flowed mainly to the regions of recent settlement outside as well as inside the British Empire. . . .

IV

But to suggest that Hobson and Lenin were mistaken in thinking that the need to export capital from Europe after 1870 was so intense that it made the colonization of most of Africa and the Pacific necessary as fields for investment is merely to throw the question open again. The essential problem remains: on what other grounds is it possible to explain this sudden expansion of European possessions, whose motive force is called imperialism?

. . . .

Looking broadly over the four centuries since the early Portuguese discoveries, it may be said that, although European motives for acquiring colonies were extremely complex, they fell into two general categories. First was the specifically economic motive, whose aim was to create a lucrative trade for the metropolitan country. Its typical expression was the trading base or factory, secured by some form of agreement with the local ruler: but, where no commodities already existed for trade, it could result in territorial possessions, like the sugar islands of the Caribbean, or the spice islands of the East; the fur-producing parts of North America, and the silver mines of Peru. The export of capital played no significant part in this economic activity, for Europe had little surplus capital before the nineteenth century, and investment was restricted to the immediate needs of trade itself, of the mines, sugar estates, etc.

By contrast, it is clear that from the earliest days of European expansion the margin between economic and other motives was small, and that many colonies were rather the product of political and military rivalries than of the desire for profit. The mercantile practices followed by all European states were as much concerned with national power as with economic advantage, and tended, as Adam Smith pointed out, to subordinate opulence to the needs of security. Indeed, by the eighteenth century, imperial policies had come to be largely a reflection of European power politics: and the struggle for territorial supremacy in America, India and the strategic bases on the route to the East were the outcome of political rather than of strictly economic competition. Britain's decision to retain Canada rather than Guadaloupe in 1763 may perhaps stand as an example of preference given to a colony offering mainly military security and prestige over one whose value was purely economic.

If, then, a general view of pre-nineteenth century imperial policies shows the complexity of its aims—made still more complicated in the early nineteenth century by the important new element of humanitarianism—it must seem surprising that Hobson should have interpreted post-1870 imperialism in narrowly economic terms, and have ignored the possibility that strictly political impulses may once again have been of major importance. The reason would seem to be that the evolution of imperial practices since about 1815 appeared, at the end of the century, to have constituted a clear break with earlier methods; to have made both the economic and the political criteria of earlier times irrelevant; and thus to have made comparison pointless. With the independence of almost all the American colonies, and the subsequent adoption by Britain—the chief remaining colonial power—of the practices of free trade, the possession of colonies no longer offered any positive economic advantage. The colonial trades were now open to all; bullion-hunting became the function of the individual prospector; and emigration, although it led to new British colonies in Australasia, flowed more naturally into the existing states of the new world. On the political side also, colonies had ceased to play an important part in diplomacy. With the preponderance of Britain as a naval power, and the weakness of most European states, power politics were largely restricted to Britain, France and Russia. As between them competitive aggressiveness was recurrent: but, except briefly in the Pacific, and more frequently in the Near East and on the borders of India, their rivalry did not produce any major competition for new territory. And this seemed to imply that the end of mercantilism had been followed by the end also of political imperialism: which in turn suggested that the renewal of a general international desire for colonies after 1870 must have sprung from some new phenomenon—the unprecedented need to acquire openings for the safe investment of surplus capital.

It is mainly because Hobson's theory of "imperialism" in his own time was based on this theory of discontinuity in nineteenth century history that it must be regarded as fallacious. For there had, in fact, been no break in the continuity of imperial development; merely a short-term variation in the methods used, corresponding with a temporary change in world conditions. In the first place, the extension of the territorial possessions of the three surviving great powers continued intermittently throughout: and the list of British acquisitions between 1840 and 1871 alone bears comparison with those of the following thirty years. On what grounds, in this period of so-called "anti-imperialism," are these to be explained? Obviously no single explanation will serve. Hong Kong stood alone as a trading base with a specifically economic function. Queensland was the result of internal expansion in Australia, British Columbia of rivalry from the United States. But the rest—the Punjab, Sind, Berar, Oudh and Lower Burma on the frontiers of British India; Basutoland, Griqualand and (temporarily) the Transvaal on the Cape frontier; and small areas round existing trading bases in West Africa—stand as evidence that an existing empire will tend always to expand its boundaries. They were not the product of an expansive British policy, but of the need for military security, for administrative efficiency, or for the protection of indigenous peoples on the frontiers of existing colonies. Basically, they demonstrated the fact, familiar in earlier centuries, that colonies which exist in a power vacuum will tend always to expand slowly until they meet with some immovable political or geographical obstacle; and that a metropolitan government can do little more than slow down the speed of movement. . . .

At the same time, it must be said that this "contiguous area" theory does not fully cover certain of the new British possessions on Hobson's list. For some of them, like East Africa, were not strictly contiguous to an existing British colony; and others, such as Nigeria or Rhodesia, were clearly annexed too suddenly and on too large a scale to be seen as the product of the domestic needs of Lagos or the Cape. These therefore suggest that some other factor was at work— competition for new colonies on political grounds—which will be considered later.

Again, in the sphere of economic policy, the antithesis between different parts of the nineteenth century were greatly exaggerated and misunderstood by Hobson. The rejection of most of the mercantile devices for stimulating European trade had not meant that trade ceased to be a matter of national concern, or that governments ceased to use political means to support their men of business; the contrast with earlier centuries lay mainly in the methods now used. Hobson seemed to think that free trade had ended "economic imperialism" of the mercantile variety simply because political control was no longer regarded as a prerequisite for economic exploitation of an undeveloped area. But, as Messrs. Gallagher and Robinson have pointed out,[5] "formal" control, as in a colony, was not the only way in which "economic imperialism" could operate; indeed, it now had two complementary features. On its specifically economic side it implied, as always, the control of the economic assets of some other country for the advantage of the metropolitan state. And the essential weapons of the European trader or financier were economic—the demand for his goods, his capital or his credit, and the effectiveness of the organization he built up in a country lacking business organization. The stranglehold he thus obtained differed only in detail from that held in the eighteenth century by British firms in the American colonies, tranferred now to the similarly defenceless, though politically independent, states of South America, the Middle and Far East. By the end of the nineteenth century most of the world had been thus brought under the economic control of European, and now also United States, business enterprise: their trade was organized and carried by foreign merchants, their revenues mortgaged to the loans they had received. This indeed was "economic imperialism" in its purest form; cosmopolitan in outlook, unconcerned with political frontiers, showing no interest in the creation of "formal" colonies except where, as in China, the formula of the open door proved otherwise unworkable. Only in the absolute volume of its activity, and in the increasing competition between rivals from newly industrialized countries, did the character of "economic imperialism" change before 1914. And, while it remained thus strictly economic and cosmopolitan, the "division of the world among the international trusts," which Lenin prophesied, remained a possibility.

Yet, even in its classical form, "economic imperialism" required political support from governments at home: and, in view of developments after about 1870, it is important to define the nature of the support it received. Essentially the men of business needed only two things which their own enterprise could not supply: a minimum standard of political security at the periphery, and the solution of the quasi-political problems arising out of their relations with foreign rivals by diplomatic action at the centre. The first need was met by the network of treaties made for them with their client countries which secured equality of opportunity and reasonable tariffs, and was backed up, where necessary, by the use of threats and force. . . . Second, and

[5] Their article, "The Imperialism of Free Trade," follows on pp. 97–111 below. [Editor's note.]

parallel with this, went the constant diplomatic work of the foreign offices of Europe in maintaining the balance between their nationals at the circumference. On the common assumption that it was to the general interest that competition should remain fair, that an artificial monopoly was to the advantage of none, and that such problems must not be allowed to harm international relations, diplomacy sought to settle these disputes without taking refuge in unilateral annexation of the area concerned. In this it was generally successful, where the will to succeed existed. . . .

It is now possible to place the imperialism of the period of Hobson's *Study* in its historical context, and to attempt a definition of the extent to which it differed from that of earlier years. The most obvious fact on which his theory was based was that, by contrast with the preceding half-century, vast areas of the world were quickly brought under European control for the first time: and it is now evident that this cannot be explained in terms of either of the two tendencies operating throughout the earlier nineteenth century. Although the break with the past was not as sharp as Hobson seemed to think, it remains true that many British annexations cannot be explained on the "contiguous area" theory: and the new possessions of France, Italy and Germany were quite definitely in a different category. But neither can these facts be explained on Hobson's theory: for, as has been said, the places now to be taken over had hitherto attracted little capital, and did not attract it in any quantity subsequently. Nor, again, can an explanation be found in the more general theory of "economic imperialism," for these places in the Pacific and in Africa for which the nations now competed were of marginal economic importance; and, on the assumptions of the past fifty years, governments might have been expected to reject demands by their nationals for annexation of territories whose administrative costs would be out of all proportion to their economic value to the nation. In sum, the most obvious facts of the new phase of imperialism cannot be explained as the logical continuation of the recent past, nor in Hobson's terms of a new economic factor. What, then, was the explanation?

An answer is not, of course, hard to find, and indeed emerges clearly from the vast literature now available. With the exception of the supporters of the "imperialism" thesis, the consensus of opinion is very marked. The new factor in imperialism was not something without precedent, certainly not anything uniquely economic, but essentially a throw-back to some of the characteristic attitudes and practices of the eighteenth century. Just as, in the early nineteenth century, the economic interests had demanded effectively that imperial questions should no longer be decided on political grounds, demanding opulence in place of security, so, at the end of the century, the balance was again reversed. The outstanding feature of the new situation was the subordination of economic to political considerations, the preoccupation with national security, military power and prestige.

Again, reasons are not hard to find. The significant fact about the years after 1870 was that Europe became once again an armed camp. The creation of a united Germany, the defeat of Austria and, above all, of France were to dominate European thinking until 1914. Between Germany and France there stood the question of Alsace-Lorraine: and for both the primary consideration was now a system of alliances which would, on the German side, prevent French counter-attack, on the French side, make revenge possible. Inevitably the rest of Europe was drawn into the politics of the balance of power between them; and for all statesmen military strength became once again the criterion of national greatness. Inevitably too this situation, with its similarities to the politics of the eighteenth century, brought in its train a return to many of the attitudes of mercantilism. Emigration to foreign states, instead of being regarded as an economic safety valve, became once again a loss of military or manufacturing manpower; and population statistics became a measure of relative national strength. Protective tariffs came back also, with the primary aim of building up national self-sufficiency and the power to make war.

Under such circumstances it was only to be expected that colonies would be regarded once again as assets in the struggle for power and status: but in fact the attitude of the powers to the imperial question was not at first a simple one. Indeed, it cannot be said that the attitudes characteristic of "the imperialism of free trade" were seriously weakened until the mid-1880's; and until then it seemed possible that the colonial question might be kept clear of European politics. This is not in fact surprising. For most of the men who then ruled Europe retained a realistic appreciation of the potential value to their countries of those parts of the world that were available for annexation. Bismarck in particular recognized that, as sources of raw materials, as fields for emigration or as spheres for trade, the areas available in Africa and the Pacific had little to offer Germany, whatever national advantages those with private interests there might claim. At best they might offer naval bases, a strictly limited trade, and bargaining counters for use in diplomacy. It is improbable that Bismarck ever really changed this opinion: and, while he held off, it was unlikely that any other power would feel strong enough to precipitate a rush for new colonies. Even Belgian and French action in the Congo failed to do this; although their ambitions showed the probable trend of future events.

It was, therefore, Bismarck's action in 1884–5, in announcing the formal control by Germany over parts of West and South West Africa, and of New Guinea, that really began the new phase of political imperialism: and it is therefore important to consider his reasons for giving Germany a "colonial policy." Was it, as Miss Townsend has argued,[6] that the pressure of the commercial interest involved in these places, and the arguments of the new colonial party in politics convinced him that colonies were an economic necessity to Germany? The answer must be that it was not. In 1884 Bismarck seems to have decided that it was time for him to stop playing the honest broker in the disputes of other powers over their own possessions—such as Egypt and the Congo—and that, on two counts, both essentially diplomatic, Germany should now stake her own claims to colonies. The first was that it was politically desirable to show France that his recent support for Britain on the Egyptian question did not imply a general hostility towards her, since he was now prepared to take action resented by Britain: the second that Britain should be made to see that German support for her in the colonial field must be repaid by closer co-operation in Europe.

In a narrow sense, then, the race for colonies was the product of diplomacy rather than of any more positive force. Germany set the example by claiming exclusive control over areas in which she had an arguable commercial stake, but no more, as a means of adding a new dimension to her international bargaining power, both in respect of what she had already taken, and of what she might claim in the future. Thereafter the process could not be checked; for, under conditions of political tension, the fear of being left out of the partition of the globe overrode all practical considerations. Perhaps Britain was the only country which showed genuine reluctance to take a share; and this was due both to her immense stake in the continuance of the *status quo* for reasons of trade, and to her continued realism in assessing the substantive value of the lands under dispute. And the fact that

---

[6] In her book, *Origins of Modern German Colonialism, 1871–1885* (New York: 1921). See her article on the subject, "Commercial and Colonial Policies of Imperial Germany," on pp. 129–139 below. [Editor's note.]

she too joined in the competition demonstrated how contagious the new political forces were. Indeed, until the end of the century, imperialism may best be seen as the extension into the periphery of the political struggle in Europe. At the centre the balance was so nicely adjusted that no positive action, no major change in the status or territory of either side was possible. Colonies thus became a means out of the impasse; sources of diplomatic strength, prestige-giving accessions of territory, hope for future economic development. New worlds were being brought into existence in the vain hope that they would maintain or redress the balance of the old.

This analysis of the dynamic force of the new imperialism has been stated in purely political terms. What part was played in it by the many non-political interests with a stake in the new colonies: the traders, the investors, the missionaries, and the speculators? For these were the most vociferous exponents of a "forward" policy in most countries: and to men like Hobson it seemed that their influence, if backed by that of the greater interest of the financier, was decisive in causing the politicians to act.

Again the problem is complex. In general terms the answer would seem to be that, while statesmen were very much aware of the pressure groups—conscious of the domestic political advantage of satisfying their demands, and often themselves sympathetic to the case they put up—they were not now, any more than earlier in the century, ready to undertake the burden of new colonies simply on their account. What made it seem as if these interests were now calling the tune was that the choice facing the statesman was no longer between annexation and the continued independence of the area in question: it was now between action and allowing a rival to step in. Salisbury and Rosebery may well have been convinced by the argument of men like Lugard that, on humanitarian grounds, it would be desirable for Britain to bring law and order to Uganda. But it was the threat of German or French occupation of the key to the Nile and Egypt that decided them to act. Yet if, in the last resort, the decision by Britain or any other country to annex was based on the highest reasons of state, it is also true that the very existence of these hitherto embarrassing pressure groups now became a diplomatic asset, since they were the obvious grounds on which valid claims could be made, an approximation to the principle of effective occupation.

Thus the relative importance of the concrete interests and demands of the various pressure groups, as compared with the political criteria

of the statesmen, was the reverse of that assigned to them by
Hobson.

. . . Yet, if the first, and territorially decisive, factor in the imperialism
of the post-1870 period was this unemotional, almost cynical, policy
of the statesmen, it cannot be said that it was the only new feature,
nor, in the long run, the' most important one. For by the time Hobson
wrote in 1902, those who supported a "forward" policy were no longer
the few diplomatic chess-players, nor even the relatively small pressure
groups, but millions of people for whom an empire had become a matter
of faith. Indeed, the rise of this imperialist ideology, this belief that
colonies were an essential attribute of any great nation, is one of the
most astonishing facts of the period. It was, moreover, an international
creed, with beliefs that seemed to differ very little from one country
to another. Its basic ideas had been clearly expressed as early as 1879
by a German, Treitschke:

Every virile people has established colonial power . . . All great nations
in the fulness of their strength have desired to set their mark upon barbarian
lands and those who fail to participate in this great rivalry will play a pitiable
role in time to come. The colonizing impulse has become a vital question
for every great nation.

By the end of the century, the "imperial idea," as it has significantly
been called, after twenty years of propaganda by such groups of en-
thusiasts as the German *Kolonialverein* and the British Imperial Federation League, had become dominant. The process of educating the
public has now been examined in detail: and it is interesting to see
that in each case the historian has found it necessary to deal almost
entirely in ideas, rather than in concrete facts. This is no accident.
The imperialism of the early twentieth century, although ironically
the product of the power politics of the previous two decades, bore
little resemblance to the ideas of men like Bismarck and Salisbury.
It was the generation of Kaiser Wilhelm II, of Theodore Roosevelt
and of Chamberlain (in his later years) that came to adopt for the
first time this mystical faith in the value of an empire. Chamberlain's
tariff campaign of 1903–5 indicates that such tenuous links as the
imperial movement had ever had with precise calculations of economic
—and even of political—advantage had now ceased to be of primary
importance.

For, by that time, imperialism had been shown to be a delusion.
It was already the common experience of all the countries that had

taken part in the partition of Africa and the Pacific that, except for the few windfalls, such as gold in West Africa, diamonds in South West Africa, and copper in the Congo and Rhodesia, the new colonies were white elephants: and that only small sectional interests in any country had obtained real benefits from them. Whether German, French, British or Italian, their trade was minute (German trade with her colonies was only ½ per cent of her external trade); their attraction for investors, except in mines, etc., was negligible; they were unsuitable for large-scale emigration, and any economic development that had taken place was usually the result of determined efforts by the European state concerned to create an artificial asset. Moreover, in most cases, the cost of administration was a dead weight on the imperial power. By 1900 all these facts were apparent and undeniable. They were constantly pressed by opponents of colonial expansion in each country; and Hobson's book consisted primarily of an exposition of these defects. Yet public opinion was increasingly oblivious to such facts: the possession of colonies had become a sacred cow, a psychological necessity. While the financiers continued to invest their money, as they had done in the previous fifty years, in economically sound projects, such as the Baghdad railway, in the non-tropical settlement colonies and independent countries, and in places like India—remaining true to the criteria of true "economic imperialism"—the politicians, pressed on now by a public demand they could not control, even if they had wanted to, continued, with increasing bellicosity, to scrape the bottom of the barrel for yet more colonial burdens for the white man to carry.

V

The reassessment of so abstract a concept as "imperialism," particularly within the present limitations of space, cannot hope to prove or to disprove anything. At the most it may lead to the suggestion that an earlier synthesis does not appear to fit the facts. How far can it be said that the arguments put forward above make necessary a revision of the theory of "imperialism" which derives from Hobson and Lenin?

The general conclusion would seem to emerge that, as an historical interpretation of the expansion of European empires between 1870 and 1914, it is unacceptable. As an economic theory it is unsatisfactory because detailed investigations have shown that the alleged need of the European investor, monopolist or individual capitalist, to find outlets for his surplus capital had little or nothing to do with the division of Africa and the Pacific between the European powers. Again, as a theory of historical development, which makes this expansion seem to be a unique phenomenon, capable of being understood only in terms of the special methodology used by Hobson and Lenin, it ignores both the continuity of nineteenth century developments, and also its similarity to earlier periods of European imperialism. In most respects, indeed, there was no break in continuity after 1870. On the political side, many of the new annexations of territory, particularly those made by Britain, resulted from the situation of existing possessions: and, on the economic side, the rapid expansion of European commercial and financial influence throughout the world—the true "economic imperialism"—did not change its character after 1870; and was no more likely then than before to have resulted in significant acquisitions of land. The real break in the continuity of nineteenth century develop-ment—the rapid extension of "formal" control over independent areas of Africa and the East—was a specifically political phenomenon in origin, the outcome of fears and rivalries within Europe. . . .

Yet, in conclusion, a paradox must be noted. Hobson's analysis of "imperialism" was defective: but the fact that it was defective was probably the result of his having grasped one essential truth about the imperial movement—that it had become irrational. Seeing clearly that the new tropical colonies could not be justified in terms of their economic value to the metropolitan powers—the criterion a nineteenth century rationalist would naturally apply—he was forced back on the theory that they must have been of value to sectional interests at least; and that these had succeeded in hoodwinking a presumably sane public opinion. Seen in this light, Hobson's sinister capitalists and their "para-sites" were nothing more than a hypothesis, a *deus ex machina*, to balance an equation between the assumed rationality of mankind and the unreasonableness of imperial policies: and the book was a plea for a return to a sane standard of values.

His mistake, then, was to think that the equation needed such artificial adjustment. For, in the second half of the twentieth century, it can be seen that imperialism owed its popular appeal not to the sinister influence of the capitalists, but to its inherent attractions for the masses. In the new quasi-democratic Europe, the popularity of the imperial idea marked a rejection of the sane morality of the account-book, and the adoption of a creed based on such irrational concepts as racial superiority and the prestige of the nation. Whether we interpret it, as did J. R. Schumpeter [in his *Imperialism and the Social Classes*] in 1919 as a castback to the ideas of the old autocratic

monarchies of the *ancien régime,* or as something altogether new—
the first of the irrational myths that have dominated the first half of
the twentieth century—it is clear that imperialism cannot be explained
in simple terms of economic theory and the nature of finance capitalism.
In its mature form it can best be described as a sociological phenomenon
with roots in political facts: and it can properly be understood only in
terms of the same social hysteria that has since given birth to other
and more disastrous forms of aggressive nationalism.

THE IMPERIALISM OF FREE TRADE *

John Gallagher and Ronald Robinson

In the last decade John Gallagher, recently appointed Beit Profes-
sor of the History of the British Commonwealth at Oxford, and
Ronald Robinson, fellow of St. John's College, Cambridge, have done
much to stimulate discussion of the origins and nature of the so-called
new imperialism. Their joint production (with Alice Denny) Africa
and the Victorians: The Official Mind of Imperialism (London and
New York; 1961) explains the "scramble" in terms of nationalist
crises within Africa and the impact of such crises on the aggressive
and insecure powers of Europe. Those who subscribe to the Hobsonian
interpretation of imperialism have taken up their cudgels against this the-
sis. In the following article the authors have tried to demolish the tradi-
tional view that the British Empire was neglected and reviled during the
mid-Victorian period, the heyday of the Manchester School which was
known for its preference for free trade over empire. Instead, the empire,
as they redefine it, increased in size and affluence at that very time,
largely through the extension of "informal" rule. Despite a sharp
counterattack by Oliver MacDonagh ["The Anti-Imperialism of Free
Trade," Economic History Review, 2d Series, XIV, No. 3 (1962), 489–
501], *the arguments of Gallagher and Robinson about the imperial*
repercussions of British industrial growth have strengthened the case
for continuity in British overseas expansion.

* Reprinted from *The Economic History Review,* 2d Series, VI, No. 1
(August, 1953), 1–4, 5–9, 10–15 with omissions, by permission of the authors
and the Economic History Society.

It ought to be a commonplace that Great Britain during the nineteenth century expanded overseas by means of "informal empire" as much as by acquiring dominion in the strict constitutional sense. For purposes of economic analysis it would clearly be unreal to define imperial history exclusively as the history of those colonies coloured red on the map. Nevertheless, almost all imperial history has been written on the assumption that the empire of formal dominion is historically comprehensible in itself and can be cut out of its context in British expansion and world politics. The conventional interpretation of the nineteenth-century empire continues to rest upon study of the formal empire alone, which is rather like judging the size and character of icebergs solely from the parts above the water-line.

.   .   .   .

The orthodox view of nineteenth-century imperial history remains that laid down from the standpoint of the racial and legalistic concept which inspired the Imperial Federation movement. Historians such as Seeley and Egerton looked on events in the formal empire as the only test of imperial activity; and they regarded the empire of kinship and constitutional dependence as an organism with its own laws of growth.[1] In this way the nineteenth century was divided into periods of imperialism and anti-imperialism, according to the extension or contraction of the formal empire and the degree of belief in the value of British rule overseas.

Ironically enough, the alternative interpretation of "imperialism," which began as part of the radical polemic against the Federationists, has in effect only confirmed their analysis. Those who have seen imperialism as the high stage of capitalism and the inevitable result of foreign investment agree that it applied historically only to the period after 1880. As a result they have been led into a similar preoccupation with formal manifestations of imperialism because the late-Victorian age was one of spectacular extension of British rule. Consequently, Hobson, Lenin, [and others] have confirmed from the opposite point of view their opponents' contention that late-Victorian imperialism was a qualitative

---

[1] The Imperial Federation League was formed in 1884 to "secure by Federation the permanent unity of the Empire." Among its leading members were Liberals like W. E. Forster and Lord Rosebery, the Conservative Edward Stanhope (appointed Colonial Secretary in 1886), and the historians J. A. Froude and Sir John Seeley. See H. E. Egerton, *Federations and Unions within the British Empire* (Oxford: 1911) and J. E. Tyler, *The Struggle for Imperial Unity: 1868–1895* (London: 1938). [Editor's note.]

change in the nature of British expansion and a sharp deviation from the innocent and static liberalism of the middle of the century. This alleged change, welcomed by one school, condemned by the other, was accepted by both.

For all their disagreement these two doctrines pointed to one interpretation; that mid-Victorian "indifference" and late-Victorian "enthusiasm" for empire were directly related to the rise and decline in free-trade beliefs. Thus Lenin wrote: "When free competition in Great Britain was at its height, i.e. between 1840 and 1860, the leading British bourgeois politicians were . . . of the opinion that the liberation of the colonies and their complete separation from Great Britain was inevitable and desirable." Professor Schuyler [in *The Fall of the Old Colonial System*, 1945] extends this to the decade from 1861 to 1870: ". . . for it was during those years that tendencies toward the disruption of the empire reached their climax. The doctrines of the Manchester school [free trade, free competition, *laissez-faire*] were at the height of their influence."

In the last quarter of the century, Professor Langer [in *The Diplomacy of Imperialism, 1890–1902*, 1935] finds that "there was an obvious danger that the British [export] market would be steadily restricted. Hence the emergence and sudden flowering of the movement for expansion. . . . Manchester doctrine had been belied by the facts. It was an outworn theory to be thrown into the discard." Their argument may be summarized in this way: the mid-Victorian formal empire did not expand, indeed it seemed to be disintegrating, therefore the period was anti-imperialist; the later-Victorian formal empire expanded rapidly, therefore this was an era of imperialism; the change was caused by the obsolescence of free trade.

The trouble with this argument is that it leaves out too many of the facts which it claims to explain. Consider the results of a decade of "indifference" to empire. Between 1841 and 1851 Great Britain occupied or annexed New Zealand, the Gold Coast, Labuan, Natal, the Punjab, Sind and Hong Kong. In the next twenty years British control was asserted over Berar, Oudh, Lower Burma and Kowloon, over Lagos and the neighbourhood of Sierra Leone, over Basutoland, Griqualand and the Transvaal; and new colonies were established in Queensland and British Columbia. Unless this expansion can be explained by "fits of absence of mind," we are faced with the paradox that it occurred despite the determination of the imperial authorities to avoid extending their rule.

This contradiction arises even if we confine our attention to the formal empire, as the orthodox viewpoint would force us to do. But if we look beyond into the regions of informal empire, then the difficulties become overwhelming. The normal account of South African policy in the middle of the century is that Britain abandoned any idea of controlling the interior. But in fact what looked like withdrawal from the Orange River Sovereignty and the Transvaal was based not on any *a priori* theories about the inconveniences of colonies but upon hard facts of strategy and commerce in a wider field. Great Britain was in South Africa primarily to safeguard the routes to the East, by preventing foreign powers from acquiring bases on the flank of those routes. In one way or another this imperial interest demanded some kind of hold upon Africa south of the Limpopo River, and although between 1852 and 1877 the Boer Republics were not controlled formally for this purpose by Britain, they were effectually dominated by informal paramountcy and by their dependence on British ports. If we refuse to narrow our view to that of formal empire, we can see how steadily and successfully the main imperial interest was pursued by maintaining supremacy over the whole region, and that it was pursued as steadily throughout the so-called anti-imperialist era as in the late-Victorian period. But it was done by shutting in the Boer Republics from the Indian Ocean: by the annexation of Natal in 1843, by keeping the Boers out of Delagoa Bay in 1860 and 1868, out of St. Lucia Bay in 1861 and 1866, and by British intervention to block the union of the two Republics under Pretorius in 1860.[2] Strangely enough it was the first Gladstone Government [1868–74] which Schuyler regards as the climax of anti-imperialism, which annexed Basutoland in 1868 and Griqualand West in 1871 in order to ensure "the safety of our South African Possessions." By informal means if possible, or by formal annexations when necessary, British paramountcy was steadily upheld.

Are these the actions of ministers anxious to preside over the liquidation of the British Empire? Do they look like "indifference" to an empire rendered superfluous by free trade? On the contrary, here is a continuity of policy which the conventional interpretation misses because it takes account only of formal methods of control. It also misses the continuous grasp of the West African coast and of the South Pacific

[2] Marthinius Pretorius (1819–1901) was elected first president of the South African Republic (1857, 1864, 1869) and was president of the Orange Free State (1859–63). After Great Britain had annexed the Orange Free State in 1877, he joined the Boer movement for independence, which achieved its goal, however briefly, three years later. [Editor's note.]

which British seapower was able to maintain. Refusals to annex are no proof of reluctance to control. As Lord Aberdeen put it in 1845: ". . . it is unnecessary to add that Her Majesty's Government will not view with indifference the assumption by another Power of a Protectorate which they, with due regard for the true interests of those [Pacific] islands, have refused."

.   .   .   .

To sum up: the conventional view of Victorian imperial history leaves us with a series of awkward questions. In the age of "anti-imperialism" why were all colonies retained? Why were so many more obtained? Why were so many new spheres of influence set up? Or again, in the age of "imperialism," as we shall see later, why was there such reluctance to annex further territory? Why did decentralization, begun under the impetus of anti-imperialism, continue? In the age of *laissez-faire* why was the Indian economy developed by the state?

These paradoxes are too radical to explain as merely exceptions which prove the rule or by concluding that imperial policy was largely irrational and inconsistent, the product of a series of accidents and chances. The contradictions, it may be suspected, arise not from the historical reality but from the historians' approach to it. A hypothesis which fits more of the facts might be that of a fundamental continuity in British expansion throughout the nineteenth century.

II

The hypothesis which is needed must include informal as well as formal expansion, and must allow for the continuity of the process. The most striking fact about British history in the nineteenth century, as Seeley pointed out, is that it is the history of an expanding society. The exports of capital and manufactures, the migration of citizens, the dissemination of the English language, ideas and constitutional forms, were all of them radiations of the social energies of the British peoples. Between 1812 and 1914 over twenty million persons emigrated from the British Isles, and nearly 70 per cent of them went outside the Empire. Between 1815 and 1880, it is estimated, £1,187,000,000 in credit had accumulated abroad, but no more than one-sixth was placed in the formal empire. Even by 1913, something less than half of the £3,975,000,000 of foreign investment lay inside the Empire. Similarly, in no year of the century did the Empire buy much more than one-third of Britain's exports. The basic fact is that British industrialization caused an ever-extending and intensifying development of overseas regions. Whether they were formally British or not, was a secondary consideration.

Imperialism, perhaps, may be defined as a sufficient political function of this process of integrating new regions into the expanding economy; its character is largely decided by the various and changing relationships between the political and economic elements of expansion in any particular region and time. Two qualifications must be made. First, imperialism may be only indirectly connected with economic integration in that it sometimes extends beyond areas of economic development, but acts for their strategic protection. Secondly, although imperialism is a function of economic expansion, it is not a necessary function. Whether imperialist phenomena show themselves or not, is determined not only by the factors of economic expansion, but equally by the political and social organization of the regions brought into the orbit of the expansive society, and also by the world situation in general.

It is only when the polities of these new regions fail to provide satisfactory conditions for commercial or strategic integration and when their relative weakness allows, that power is used imperialistically to adjust those conditions. Economic expansion, it is true, will tend to flow into the regions of maximum opportunity, but maximum opportunity depends as much upon political considerations of security as upon questions of profit. Consequently, in any particular region, if economic opportunity seems large but political security small, then full absorption into the extending economy tends to be frustrated until power is exerted upon the state in question. Conversely, in proportion as satisfactory political frameworks are brought into being in this way, the frequency of imperialist intervention lessens and imperialist control is correspondingly relaxed. It may be suggested that this willingness to limit the use of paramount power to establishing security for trade is the distinctive feature of the British imperialism of free trade in the nineteenth century, in contrast to the mercantilist use of power to obtain commercial supremacy and monopoly through political possession.

On this hypothesis the phasing of British expansion or imperialism is not likely to be chronological. Not all regions will reach the same level of economic integration at any one time; neither will all regions need the same type of political control at any one time. As the British industrial revolution grew, so new markets and sources of supply were linked to it at different times, and the degree of imperialist action accompanying that process varied accordingly. Thus mercantilist techniques of formal empire were being employed to develop India in the mid-Victorian age at the same time as informal techniques of free trade were being used in Latin America for the same purpose. It is for this reason that attempts to make phases of imperialism correspond directly to phases in the economic growth of the metropolitan economy are likely to prove in vain. The fundamental continuity of British expansion is only obscured by arguing that changes in the terms of trade or in the character of British exports necessitated a sharp change in the process.

From this vantage point the many-sided expansion of British industrial society can be viewed as a whole of which both the formal and informal empires are only parts. Both of them then appear as variable political functions of the extending pattern of overseas trade, investment, migration and culture. If this is accepted, it follows that formal and informal empire are essentially interconnected and to some extent interchangeable. Then not only is the old, legalistic, narrow idea of empire unsatisfactory, but so is the old idea of informal empire as a separate, non-political category of expansion. A concept of informal empire which fails to bring out the underlying unity between it and the formal empire is sterile. Only within the total framework of expansion is nineteenth-century empire intelligible. So we are faced with the task of re-fashioning the interpretations resulting from defective concepts of organic constitutional empire on the one hand and Hobsonian "imperialism" on the other.

The economic importance—even the pre-eminence—of informal empire in this period has been stressed often enough. What was overlooked was the inter-relation of its economic and political arms; how political action aided the growth of commercial supremacy, and how this supremacy in turn strengthened political influence. In other words, it is the politics as well as the economics of the informal empire which we have to include in the account. Historically, the relationship between these two factors has been both subtle and complex. It has been by no means a simple case of the use of gunboats to demolish a recalcitrant state in the cause of British trade. The type of political lien between the expanding economy and its formal or informal dependencies, as might be expected, has been flexible. In practice it has tended to vary with the economic value of the territory, the strength of its political structure, the readiness of its rulers to collaborate with British commercial or strategic purposes, the ability of the native society to undergo economic change without external control, the extent to which domestic and foreign political situations permitted British intervention, and, finally, how far European rivals allowed British policy a free hand.

Accordingly, the political lien has ranged from a vague, informal paramountcy to outright political possession; and, consequently, some of these dependent territories have been formal colonies whereas others have not. The difference between formal and informal empire has not been one of fundamental nature but of degree. The ease with which a region has slipped from one status to the other helps to confirm this. Within the last two hundred years, for example, India has passed from informal to formal association with the United Kingdom and, since World War II, back to an informal connexion. Similarly, British West Africa has passed through the first two stages and seems to-day likely to follow India into the third.

III

Let us now attempt, tentatively, to use the concept of the totality of British expansion described above to restate the main themes of the history of modern British expansion. We have seen that interpretations of this process fall into contradictions when based upon formal political criteria alone. If expansion both formal and informal is examined as a single process, will these contradictions disappear?

The growth of British industry made new demands upon British policy. It necessitated linking undeveloped areas with British foreign trade and, in so doing, moved the political arm to force an entry into markets closed by the power of foreign monopolies.

British policy . . . was active in this way before the American colonies had been lost, but its greatest opportunities came during the Napoleonic Wars. The seizure of the French and Spanish West Indies, the filibustering expedition to Buenos Aires in 1806, the taking of Java in 1811, were all efforts to break into new regions and to tap new resources by means of political action. But the policy went further than simple house-breaking, for once the door was opened and British imports with their political implications were pouring in, they might stop the door from being shut again. Raffles, for example, temporarily broke the Dutch monopoly of the spice trade in Java and opened the island to free trade. Later, he began the informal British paramountcy over the Malacca trade routes and the Malay peninsula by founding Singapore. In South America, at the same time, British policy was aiming at indirect political hegemony over new regions for the purposes of trade. The British navy carried the Portuguese royal family to Brazil after the breach with Napoleon, and the British representative there extorted from his grateful clients the trade treaty of 1810 which left British imports paying a lower tariff than the goods of the mother country. The thoughtful stipulation was added "that the Present Treaty shall be unlimited in point of duration, and that the obligations and conditions expressed or implied in it shall be perpetual and immutable." . . .

In both the formal and informal dependencies in the mid-Victorian age there was much effort to open the continental interiors and to extend the British influence inland from the ports and to develop the hinterlands. The general strategy of this development was to convert these areas into complementary satellite economies, which would provide raw materials and food for Great Britain, and also provide widening markets for its manufactures. This was the period, the orthodox interpretation would have us believe, in which the political arm of expansion was dormant or even withered. In fact, that alleged inactivity is seen to be a delusion if we take into account the development in the informal aspect. Once entry had been forced into Latin America, China and the Balkans, the task was to encourage stable governments as good investment risks, just as in weaker or unsatisfactory states it was considered necessary to coerce them into more co-operative attitudes.

. . . .

The types of informal empire and the situations it attempted to exploit were as various as the success which it achieved. Although commercial and capital penetration tended to lead to political co-operation and hegemony, there are striking exceptions. In the United States, for example, British business turned the cotton South into a colonial economy, and the British investor hoped to do the same with the Mid-West. But the political strength of the country stood in his way. It was impossible to stop American industrialization, and the industrialized sections successfully campaigned for tariffs, despite the opposition of those sections which depended on the British trade connexion. In the same way, American political strength thwarted British attempts to establish Texas, Mexico and Central America as informal dependencies.

Conversely, British expansion sometimes failed, if it gained political supremacy without effecting a successful commercial penetration. There were spectacular exertions of British policy in China, but they did little to produce new customers. Britain's political hold upon China failed to break down Chinese economic self-sufficiency. The Opium War of 1840, the renewal of war in 1857, widened the inlets for British trade but they did not get Chinese exports moving. Their main effect was an unfortunate one from the British point of view, for such foreign pressures put Chinese society under great strains as the Taiping Rebellion unmistakably showed. It is important to note that this weakness was regarded in London as an embarrassment, and not as a lever for extracting further concessions. In fact, the British worked to prop up the tottering Pekin regime, for as Lord Clarendon put it in 1870, "British interests in China are strictly commercial, or at all events only so far political as they may be for the protection of commerce." The value of this self-denial became clear in the following decades when the Pekin government, threatened with a scramble for China, leaned more and more on the diplomatic support of the honest British broker.

The simple recital of these cases of economic expansion, aided and abetted by political action in one form or other, is enough to expose the inadequacy of the conventional theory that free trade could dispense with empire. We have seen that it did not do so. Economic expansion in the mid-Victorian age was matched by a corresponding political expansion which has been overlooked because it could not be seen by that study of maps which, it has been said, drives sane men mad. It is absurd to deduce from the harmony between London and the colonies of white settlement in the mid-Victorian age any British reluctance to intervene in the fields of British interests. The warships at Canton are as much a part of the period as responsible government for Canada; the battlefields of the Punjab are as real as the abolition of suttee.

Far from being an era of "indifference," the mid-Victorian years were the decisive stage in the history of British expansion overseas, in that the combination of commercial penetration and political influence allowed the United Kingdom to command those economies which could be made to fit best into her own. A variety of techniques adapted to diverse conditions and beginning at different dates were employed to effect this domination. A paramountcy was set up in Malaya centred on Singapore; a suzerainty over much of West Africa reached out from the port of Lagos and was backed up by the African squadron. On the east coast of Africa British influence at Zanzibar, dominant thanks to the exertions of Consul Kirk, placed the heritage of Arab command on the mainland at British disposal.

But perhaps the most common political technique of British expansion was the treaty of free trade and friendship made with or imposed upon a weaker state. The treaties with Persia of 1836 and 1857, the Turkish treaties of 1838 and 1861, the Japanese treaty of 1858, the favours extracted from Zanzibar, Siam and Morocco, the hundreds of anti-slavery treaties signed with crosses by African chiefs—all these treaties enabled the British government to carry forward trade with these regions.

Even a valuable trade with one region might give place to a similar trade with another which could be more easily coerced politically. The Russian grain trade, for example, was extremely useful to Great Britain. But the Russians' refusal to hear of free trade, and the British inability to force them into it, caused efforts to develop the grain of the Ottoman empire instead, since British pressure at Constantinople had been able to hustle the Turk into a liberal trade policy. The dependence of the commercial thrust upon the political arm resulted in a general tendency for British trade to follow the invisible flag of informal empire.

Since the mid-Victorian age now appears as a time of large-scale expansion, it is necessary to revise our estimate of the so-called "imperialist" era as well. Those who accept the concept of "economic imperialism" would have us believe that the annexations at the end of the century represented a sharp break in policy, due to the decline of free trade, the need to protect foreign investment, and the conversion of statesmen to the need for unlimited land-grabbing. All these explanations are questionable. In the first place, the tariff policy of Great Britain did not change. Again, British foreign investment was no new thing and most of it was still flowing into regions outside the formal empire. Finally the statesmen's conversion to the policy of extensive annexation was partial, to say the most of it. Until 1887, and only occasionally after that date, party leaders showed little more enthusiasm for extending British rule than the mid-Victorians. Salisbury was infuriated by the "superficial philanthropy" and "roguery" of the "fanatics " who advocated expansion. When pressed to aid the missions in Nyasaland in 1888, he retorted: "It is not our duty to do it. We should be risking tremendous sacrifices for a very doubtful gain." After 1888, Salisbury, Rosebery and Chamberlain [3] accepted the scramble for Africa

[3] 3rd Marquess of Salisbury (1830–1903), leader of the Conservative party after Disraeli's death in 1881, was prime minister three times (1885–86, 1886–92, 1895–1902) and foreign secretary during most of his administrations (as well as 1878–80). Archibald Philip Primrose, 5th Earl of Rosebery (1847–1929), Liberal foreign secretary under Gladstone (1886, 1892–94), became prime minister for a year (1894–95). Rosebery led the imperialist faction within the Liberal party. [Editor's note.]

as a painful but unavoidable necessity which arose from a threat of foreign expansion and the irrepressible tendency of trade to overflow the bounds of empire, dragging the government into new and irksome commitments. But it was not until 1898 that they were sufficiently confident to undertake the reconquest of so vital a region as the Sudan.

Faced with the prospect of foreign acquisitions of tropical territory hitherto opened to British merchants, the men in London resorted to one expedient after another to evade the need of formal expansion and still uphold British paramountcy in those regions. British policy in the late, as in the mid-Victorian period, preferred informal means of extending imperial supremacy rather than direct rule. Throughout the two alleged periods the extension of British rule was a last resort—and it is this preference which has given rise to the many "anti-expansionist" remarks made by Victorian ministers. What these much quoted expressions obscure, is that in practice mid-Victorian as well as late-Victorian policy makers did not refuse to extend the protection of formal rule over British interests when informal methods had failed to give security. The fact that informal techniques were more often sufficient for this purpose in the circumstances of the mid-century than in the later period when the foreign challenge to British supremacy intensified, should not be allowed to disguise the basic continuity of policy. Throughout, British governments worked to establish and maintain British paramountcy by whatever means best suited the circumstances of their diverse regions of interest. The aims of the mid-Victorians were no more "anti-imperialist" than their successors', though they were more often able to achieve them informally; and the late-Victorians were no more "imperialist" than their predecessors, even though they were driven to annex more often. British policy followed the principle of extending control informally if possible and formally if necessary. To label the one method "anti-imperialist" and the other "imperialist," is to ignore the fact that whatever the method British interests were steadily safeguarded and extended. The usual summing up of the policy of the free trade empire as "trade not rule" should read "trade with informal control if possible; trade with rule when necessary." This statement of the continuity of policy disposes of the over-simplified explanation of

---

Joseph Chamberlain (1836–1914), a versatile Radical politician, was regarded as a contender for the Liberal party leadership until his break with Gladstone, ostensibly over the issue of Irish Home Rule. An active social reformer and imperial expansionist, Chamberlain joined Lord Salisbury's cabinet in 1895 as Colonial Secretary and became deeply involved in South African troubles as well as in the agitation for tariff reform. [Editor's note.]

involuntary expansion inherent in the orthodox interpretation based on the discontinuity between the two periods.

One principle then emerges plainly: it is only when and where informal political means failed to provide the framework of security for British enterprise (whether commercial, or philanthropic or simply strategic) that the question of establishing formal empire arose. In satellite regions peopled by European stock, in Latin America or Canada, for instance, strong governmental structures grew up; in totally non-European areas, on the other hand, expansion unleashed such disruptive forces upon the indigenous structures that they tended to wear out and even collapse with use. This tendency in many cases accounts for the extension of informal British responsibility and eventually for the change from indirect to direct control.

It was in Africa that this process of transition manifested itself most strikingly during the period after 1880. Foreign loans and predatory bankers by the 1870's had wrecked Egyptian finances and were tearing holes in the Egyptian political fabric. The Anglo-French dual financial control, designed to safeguard the foreign bondholders and to restore Egypt as a good risk, provoked anti-European feeling. With the revolt of Arabi Pasha in 1881, the Khedive's government could serve no longer to secure either the all-important Canal or the foreign investors' pound of flesh.

The motives for the British occupation of 1882 were confused and varied; the desire, evident long before Disraeli's purchase of shares, to dominate the Canal; the interests of the bondholders; and the over-anxiety to forestall any foreign power, especially France, from taking advantage of the prevailing anarchy in Egypt to interpose its power across the British road to India. Nearly all Gladstone's Cabinet admitted the necessity of British intervention, although for different reasons, and, in order to hold together his distracted ministry, the Prime Minister agreed.

The British expedition was intended to restore a stable Egyptian government under the ostensible rule of the Khedive and inside the orbit of informal British influence. When this was achieved, the army, it was intended, should be withdrawn. But the expedition had so crushed the structure of Egyptian rule that no power short of direct British force could make it a viable and trustworthy instrument of informal hegemony and development. Thus the Liberal Government following its plan, which had been hastily evolved out of little more than ministerial disagreements, drifted into the prolonged occupation of

Egypt it was intent on avoiding. In fact, the occupying power became directly responsible for the defence, the debts and development of the country. The perverse effect of British policy was gloomily summed up by Gladstone: "We have done our Egyptian business and we are an Egyptian government." Egypt, then, is a striking example of an informal strategy misfiring due to the undermining of the satellite state by investment and by pseudo-nationalist reaction against foreign influence.

The Egyptian question, in so far as it was closely bound with the routes to India and the defence of the Indian empire itself, was given the highest priority by British policy in the 'eighties and 'nineties. In order to defend the spinal cord of British trade and empire, tropical African and Pacific claims were repeatedly sacrificed as pawns in the higher game. In 1884, for example, the Foreign Office decided that British vulnerability in Egypt made it unwise to compete with foreign powers in the opening scramble for West Africa; and it was therefore proposed ". . . to confine ourselves to securing the utmost possible freedom of trade on that [west] coast, yielding to others the territorial responsibilities . . . and seeking compensation on the east coast . . . where the political future of the country is of real importance to Indian and imperial interests." British policy was not one of indiscriminate land-grabbing. And, indeed, the British penetration into Uganda and their securing of the rest of the Nile Valley was a highly selective programme, in so far as it surrendered some British West African claims to France and transferred part of East Africa to Germany.

IV

Thus the mid-Victorian period now appears as an era of large-scale expansion, and the late-Victorian age does not seem to introduce any significant novelty into that process of expansion. The annexations of vast undeveloped territories, which have been taken as proof that this period alone was the great age of expansion, now pale in significance, at least if our analysis is anywhere near the truth. That the area of direct imperial rule was extended is true, but is it the most important or characteristic development of expansion during this period? The simple historical fact that Africa was the last field of European penetration is not to say that it was the most important; this would be a truism were it not that the main case of the Hobson school is founded on African examples. On the other hand, it is our main contention that the process of expansion had reached its most valuable targets long before the ex-

ploitation of so peripheral and marginal a field as tropical Africa. Consequently arguments, founded on the technique adopted in scrambling
for Africa, would seem to be of secondary importance.

Therefore, the historian who is seeking to find the deepest meaning
of the expansion at the end of the nineteenth century should look not
at the mere pegging out of claims in African jungles and bush, but at
the successful exploitation of the empire, both formal and informal,
which was then coming to fruition in India, in Latin America, in
Canada and elsewhere. The main work of imperialism in the so-called
expansionist era was in the more intensive development of areas already
linked with the world economy, rather than in the extensive annexations of the remaining marginal regions of Africa. The best finds and
prizes had already been made; in tropical Africa the imperialists were
merely scraping the bottom of the barrel.

THE ORIGINS OF THE NEW FRENCH
EMPIRE *

H. Brunschwig

*The motives underlying the expansion of France's second colonial
empire have provoked much controversy. Were the colonies acquired
for reasons of state, in the interests of bondholders, to satisfy the needs
of French industry, or in response to an overpowering impulse to spread
French civilization? Henri Brunschwig has addressed himself to this
problem in his stimulating book,* Mythes et réalités de l'impérialisme
colonial français, 1871–1914 *(Paris: 1960). In the following selection
from this study, Professor Brunschwig presents strong evidence to show
that French colonial expansion was originally motivated by the desire
for prestige. Later, colonies were justified in terms of national security.
But since the case for empire was supported neither by popular sentiment nor by economic self-interest, the French public had to be edu-*

---

* Reprinted from Mythes et réalités de l'impérialisme colonial français, 1871–
1914 (Paris: 1960), pp. 10–16, 19, 21–28, with omissions, by permission of
Librairie Armand Colin. Copyright 1960 by Max Leclerc et Cie, Proprietors of
Librairie Armand Colin. Translated from the original by E. D. and G. H. Nadel.

cated to think in imperial terms. This was done under the Third Republic; Professor Brunschwig tells us how it was done and by whom. The author is Director of L'Ecole Pratique des Hautes Etudes and Professor at both the Institut des Hautes Etudes d'Outre-Mer and the Institut des Sciences Politiques. Among his other works are La Colonisation française and L'Expansion allemande outre-mer.

The French Policy of Prestige

The colonial policy of France was quite unlike that of other countries. It is true that, like the others, she had adopted the system of plantations, but from the first her attitude to colonial matters had been different from that of England, the Netherlands, Portugal, and even Spain. It had not been the search for profit which had led the kings of France to found overseas establishments. The wish for prestige, rather than for commercial gain, explains their colonial policy. They could not admit that the sun set every night on their lands, while it never set on the domains of the kings of Spain. The aim of the foreign policy of Richelieu was to augment the grandeur and the glory of the King, and that grandeur was made up as much of "dignity," of moral prestige, as of material power. Richelieu wrote in his Mémoires, in 1622, that the Queen, mother of Louis XIII, "put it to the King continually that, being the first King in dignity, he should prevent the King of Spain from being the first King in power." Dignity had required that "New Frances" appear in the New World, beside the New Spain and the New Castille. The material profits gained from these establishments was slight, and, even from the moral point of view, the glory given by the possession of the Antilles or Canada could not evidently compare to that accruing from the acquisition of Trois Evêchés or of Alsace. The colonial policy of France, in its origins, was explained rather by the search for prestige than for profit, but it remained subsidiary and was subordinated to the continental policy, which alone made for great, successful achievements.

"People the new lands with French and Catholic colonists, by means of large Chartered Companies. Do this in order to build up the political and commercial grandeur of France against Spain and to 'serve the interests of God'—such seemed to be the formula for colonial action in the first half of the seventeenth century," Léon Deschamps justly wrote in 1891.

In the first half of the seventeenth century, sugar cane was introduced into the Antilles, followed soon by black slaves. The plantation was born. The profits which the colonials and the shipowners drew from this and the efforts of Colbert to control foreign trade and to develop the Royal Navy created the policy of "excluding" others, already practiced to varying extent by foreign countries. And, as in foreign countries, the system gave full satisfaction to its users. For more than a century, the shipowners of Atlantic ports developed their businesses, and the colonists enriched themselves likewise. Modern cities, bright and elegant, conceived according to carefully elaborated plans, with shaded promenades, squares of harmonious proportions, fountains and gardens, space and light were built at Lorient, La Rochelle, Nantes, and Bordeaux.

The system functioned so well in the middle of the eighteenth century that the *philosophes* and the diplomats forgot the political interest with which colonization had for a long time been invested. Montesquieu, the Encyclopedists, Choiseul, and others were pleased to repeat that the colonies had no other object but to promote trade. If trade lagged, the colony could easily be abandoned. No one had the impression of a national failure when in the Treaty of Paris in 1763 France ceded Canada, which had no colonial products, to the English. But the negotiators of this treaty relentlessly defended the right of France to trade in Senegal, the only producer of gum. In the eighteenth century, colonies were no longer important elements in French prestige. It was in Europe that one acquired prestige, in Europe only that one could lose face.

This trade policy was not criticized in France, as it was in England, primarily because French colonists were much less numerous and would not have been capable of subsisting without the metropolis. Their protestations against excessive prices and the poor quality of the goods which the shipowners sold them, against the abuses or the incompetence of certain officials, against the continual high prices of slaves, and the declining yield of a soil exhausted by too intensive cultivation did not shake the system. It was not a question of abolishing it, but only of changing it. On the eve of the Revolution, this system, founded on commercial monopoly, slavery, and sugar cane was generally considered useful to the nation. And it gave to the shipowners and planters a security which their descendants would for a long time remember with nostalgia.

Meanwhile, in the course of the Revolution and the Empire, France lost all her overseas territories. The French realized then that they did not need them. It was not the nation which was ruined, but only the small group of shipowners, merchants, and planters which made the system function. The mass of Frenchmen had time to accustom themselves to having no more colonies.

In the course of the same period, the foundations on which the system had been built crumbled. France had had to undertake at the Treaty of Vienna of 1815 to renounce the slave trade, with a period of grace of six years. Beet sugar, propagated under the Empire, competed keenly with cane sugar throughout Europe; the latter had ceased to be the precious commodity, comparable to foreign exchange in our modern finance, which it is always advantageous to export. The other colonial products could easily be acquired at less cost than that required by the system of plantations. And even if this system had not disappeared, the new markets of Latin America, the new lands of Oceania, and the greater part of the African coast were now freely available to anyone's initiative.

Under these conditions, one wonders whether France was right to want to recoup her old colonies. In point of fact, she only resolved to do it for motives of prestige. When in 1816 the Portuguese delayed giving back Guiana which they had occupied, the Duke of Richelieu wrote to the French ambassador in London:

You perceive perfectly that it would be impossible to accede to the demands of Portugal, less because of the real interest that exists for us to keep a territory which cannot offer real advantages except in the far distant future, than because the dignity of the King and of the State would be injured by a concession which would not be justified by any law whatever on the part of Portugal. This consideration is of the greatest necessity, because, in our present situation, any act of concession would be taken for weakness.

The liberals and the agrarians proposed repeatedly—through their Deputies—a reduction in the financial supplies which the government claimed for the colonies. Their criticisms remind one, sometimes, of those of English liberals. General Foy explained, in 1822, that the colonies were without utility in time of peace and dangerous in time of war:

"Calculate the outlays which we make for the Navy in order to protect our foreign trade; would they not be more usefully employed for our agriculture, to make our domestic trade more active and to develop our industry?"

In 1829 the Deputy Bessières declared: "For what our colonies are worth to us and cost us, we would gain much more by not having them. The colonial system, once advantageous, is now no longer practicable. I say that it has incontestably ceased to be necessary."

These critics, however, found no echo in public opinion. They always met with the same response: no navy without colonies.

.   .   .   .

The navy, the necessity for which was not disputed, the fleet, which was progressively rebuilt under King Louis-Philippe, represented above all the effort to re-establish the prestige of France vis-à-vis England. Colonial policy, which in England satisfied commercial needs, was in France only one aspect of the domestic or foreign policy of governments worried about their popularity. This concern appeared from one end of this period to the other.

The French navy collaborated half-heartedly with the English in the repression of the trade in Negroes. The rural masses had no strong feelings in favor of emancipation of the slaves, probably because the anti-slavery campaign was led by lay intellectuals (whereas in England it was intimately connected with the Wesleyan religious revival). If the Abbé Grégoire [1] had not been a former constitutional priest, suspect under the Restoration, if he had stayed in the hierarchy and had enjoyed the confidence of his superiors, he would have been able to lead the Church into his crusade in favor of the Negroes. The French people would thus have become deeply affected and as stirred up as the English people; the economic interests allied to slavery which would have been an obstacle to this movement were certainly weaker in France than in England. But the Abbé Grégoire was a tainted outsider, and the cause of the Negroes remained in the hands of distinguished lawyers to whom the people in the hinterlands did not listen. . . .

As to the merchants, their participation was ephemeral and sporadic. They interested themselves in certain points on the western coast of Africa just when the navy became anxious to imitate the English, whose influence was growing on the Gold Coast and whose geographers were exploring the course of the Niger. De Bouët-Willaumetz was eventually charged with acquiring some concessions on the Gulf of Guinea; Assinies, Garroway, king Denis, with his drum-major baton and

[1] Abbé Grégoire (1750–1831): the "regicide" Bishop of Blois who in 1792 had been foremost among those urging the abolition of monarchy and the prosecution of Louis XVI. An ardent republican he sat in the Constituent Assembly (1789), the National Convention (1792), the Council of Five Hundred (1795), and the Senate (1801). His election to the Lower Chamber in 1819 alarmed the Royalists and provoked a minor political crisis. [Editor's note.]

his *légion d'honneur*—these names and these pictures entered into French school-books and stayed there. In fact, the establishments acquired between 1839 and 1842 merely vegetated.

.   .   .   .

France did not need land like England. It was by hundreds of individuals and not by tens of thousands that one counted the French emigrants to the colonies in the course of this period. The only important conquests effected before 1870, Algeria, Senegal, Cochin-China, did not result from a mercantilist or imperialist doctrine. They are explained completely by the contingencies of domestic or foreign policy and had no profound effect on public opinion. Algeria alone provoked numerous polemics. The disappointments there over half a century contributed to making unpopular in France a colonial policy, the need for which did not exist. Colonies, which were of second-rate importance in French economic life, did not figure among the essential factors of the national patrimony; the governments, without invoking, like the English, political or economic doctrines or moral principles, often hesitated to keep them. They sought to "restrain" the occupation of Algeria between 1830 and 1840, lost interest in Senegal between 1828 and 1852, had to evacuate Cochin-China between 1862 and 1864, and effectively abandoned the Ivory Coast in 1871.

The anxiety about prestige explains why one hardly ever wondered, in France, in contrast with English doctrine, if the colonies were profitable. Undoubtedly if one tried to tabulate receipts and expenditures for the French colonies between 1815 and 1870, the latter would appear to have made for a considerable deficit. But that was not the question. The colonies did not have to be sources of income. Their role was to dispute with England the mastery of the seas, to affirm before the world the presence, the grandeur, and the expansion of France. It was normal that this had to be paid for like all expenses of sovereignty.

The Anglo-French treaty of commerce of 1860 enabled France to enter into the orbit of free trade. The industrialists protested at first, then adapted themselves to it, and, at the beginning of the Third Republic, everyone was satisfied. Besides, free trade reigned unchallenged over all of Europe. In France at this moment, colonies stood for failures and burdens more than successes, and no one would have ventured to encourage further expeditions to far-off places.

The paradoxes, it is apparent, were reciprocal: the English acquired an empire at the time when they proclaimed that colonies were, on the whole, detrimental to their economy. They preferred to do business under a policy of free trade. The French conquered an empire when their overseas trade had been most reduced and when their population showed not the slightest interest in a wider world.

Nationalism

Nationalism arose and spread in Europe at the same time as liberalism. . . .

The French had every reason to satisfy their hunger for nationalism in 1815. They had, for close to a generation, decided the fortunes of others as well as their own. They had been conquered finally, but the treaties of 1815 respected their independence. Of the three constituent elements of nationalism, individual civic conscience, collective will to form a nation state, and national pride, none had been stifled.

In the course of the century, until 1870, nationalism was not, in France, the dominant characteristic of the masses. If it expressed itself violently during short-lived crises like that in 1840, it was quickly forgotten. It did not bring into being active political organizations, secret or otherwise, as in Germany, Italy, and Poland. In brief, nobody lost any sleep over it. The specific characteristic of the French was rather their wish to preserve the conquests of the Revolution, to impede the return of despotism, and to encourage the spread of a liberal regime, of a bourgeoisie with peasant roots, while facilitating upward social mobility by means of progressive evolution towards democracy. . . .

This attachment of the French to a middle-class and liberal society could have lasted a long time if the year 1870–1871 had not profoundly modified the moral equilibrium of Europe. While their successes pushed the Italians and the Germans to prefer new conquests to social or political reforms, the French were humiliated. The principles of 1789, the right to self-determination, had been violated. The body of France had been amputated. The theme of revenge arose. At the moment when the Third Republic gratified to the full the wishes of the traditional liberal opposition, nationalism awakened. The new men who guided the state took care to avoid any further mortifications. They shared with the intellectual elite the wish to prove that France had not fallen, that she remained a great power. They sought to restore and to increase her prestige in all areas.

Victories and defeats thus imbued the peoples of the Continent with a bellicose nationalism which had never been so widespread or so passionate. This nationalism soon extended to the overseas territories. The extension was immediate in Italy, which stretched out into Tunis:

geography and history seemed to impose its recovery [by the French].
The French themselves thought, in general, that colonial expeditions
turned the country away from revenge, which should be her only preoccupation. Many of them had participated in the humanitarian movement and were all the more hostile to colonial expansion which seemed
to them to have miscarried, especially in Algeria. In order for their
traditional hostility to disappear, a revision of the generally received
theses had to be undertaken. It was principally the geographers who
devoted themselves to this task.

Origins of French Colonial Imperialism

The Geographic Society of France, founded in 1821, never had
more than 300 members until 1860. It had 780 in 1873 and 2,000 in
1881. Between 1871 and 1881 eleven other geographic societies were
created in the provinces. In 1881, all the French societies combined had
9,500 members compared to the 30,000 which was the total for the geographic societies of the world. The first international congress for geography was held at Antwerp in 1871. The second met at Paris in 1875.

The Royal Geographic Society of London had enjoyed a principal
role in the progress of global exploration since the beginning of the
century. It had never been involved in politics or religion. Science alone
had always dominated its activities. The French geographers showed,
after 1871, slightly different preoccupations. In a report of 1873, the
secretary general of the Society of Paris, Charles Maunoir, noted: "It is
dangerous for a people to be indifferent to conditions of other peoples
and to be ignorant of resources offered by lands far from their own commercial and colonial activities." And the president, La Roncière le
Noury, who had put the Society in touch with the Chamber of Commerce of Paris, declared in a short speech in 1874: "Abstract science,
Gentlemen, is not sufficient for Humanity. Science is not really fecund
unless it is an instrument of progress and production. It is not only in
the interest of curiosity that successive geographic explorations and discoveries have been made. The discovery of America, the persevering
explorations in the interior of Africa, the search for a passage towards
the North Pole had, besides a scientific aim, a political and commercial
object."

The following year, in inaugurating the international congress for
geography in the presence of the President of the Republic, MacMahon,
he proclaimed:

Gentlemen, Providence has dictated to us the obligation to know the earth and to conquer it. This supreme commandment is one of the most imperative duties inscribed in our intelligence and in our activities. Geography, that science which inspires such great devotion and in the name of which so many victims have been sacrificed, has become the philosophy of the world.

Preceding the Society of Paris, a Commercial Geographic Society was created at Bordeaux in 1874; its founder, Foncin, explained that he saw there a means of "rehabilitating" France.

.   .   .   .

The secretary general of the Society of Valenciennes, Bébin, explained in 1881 that France, obliged to restrict herself greatly in Europe, must turn toward the colonies:

There, the living forces of the nation, which are beginning to realize their confinement in the narrow limits of the Treaty of Frankfurt [1871], would be capable of accomplishing a complete expansion, without anyone being in a position to foresee—once the events we desire have come about— where our flag will come to rest one day . . . To remain a great nation or to become one, a people must colonize.

The same ideas are found again in the magnificent publication of Francis Garnier who accompanied Doudart de Lagrée in the exploration of the Mekong and directed the expedition after the death of his chief in 1868. The *Voyage d'exploration en Indo-Chine* appeared in 1873. The author lamented the abstention of France, which lived "retired within itself." He deplored French policy in China which was always subordinated to that of England. He invoked the civilizing mission of France, and "if he appealed as much to economic motives, his ardent enthusiasm arose from his faith in destiny, from his consuming personal ambition, from the urgency he felt to raise the prestige of his country, and from his keen awareness of the rivalry with England."

One could multiply the examples and the citations. They would always disclose the same themes: rehabilitation of conquered France, civilizing mission, development of trade, colonial expansion.

These slogans which dailies like *Le Journal des Débats*, periodicals like *La Revue géographique, Revue des deux Mondes,* and lecturers spread widely had something surprising about them. The fact is that France's colonial trade was negligible; moreover, free trade had done away with the obstacles capable of impeding the development of her trade with foreign nations. It was a fact also that colonial expansion had never been popular because emigration had never been necessary. Finally, it was a fact that these geographers and economists who preached the development of trade were, for the most part, intellectuals, government men, functionaries—and not those most interested, namely, the merchants, who had no reason to complain. We shall see that the economic circles had not encouraged the first colonial expeditions of the Third Republic. They did not push intervention in Tonkin in 1873, or the action in Tunis in 1880, or the exploration of Central Africa.

New men, who in politics and in literature wanted to prove to the world that France was not defeated, strove to convince these economic circles. They did it by revising the traditional conceptions of colonization. The credit for this goes mainly to Paul Leroy-Beaulieu, whose ideas were pondered throughout the continent. The prize-winning dissertation which he presented in 1870 to the Academy of Moral and Political Sciences on a question put to the meeting four years earlier appeared in 1874 under the title: *De la colonisation chez les peuples modernes.* The young laureate was then thirty-one years old. Born of an upper middle-class family of parliamentarians, he married the daughter of Michel Chevalier in 1870. He was elected in 1878 to the Academy of Moral and Political Sciences and in 1879 succeeded his father-in-law as Professor of Moral and Political Sciences at the Collège de France. He was, one can see, one of the most brilliant of these "notables," sponsors of the Third Republic who worked hard to confer on it as much prestige and dignity as the monarchies of Europe enjoyed.

The great novelty of Leroy-Beaulieu's book was the distinction which he established between settlement colonies, like the British Dominions, and colonies for capital investment. The first, he thought, were out of date: the earliest wave of people emigrating without profit for the metropolis. A great country gained nothing by creating settlement colonies. And on this point the liberal English doctrine furnished the author with arguments that had been unrefuted for three generations. But there was another form of colonization, that which developed somewhat anarchically in Tunis and in Egypt, and in respect to which a doctrine had not yet been elaborated. Emigration should be directed towards regions where capital could be invested for the greater profit of their inhabitants as well as the financial backers:

The greatest utility of colonies . . . is to give the commerce of the metropolis large scope, to activate and to maintain its industry and to provide the inhabitants of the mother country, manufacturers, workers and consumers, with an increase in profits, in salaries or in possessions. The entire world will profit from it, for it is not a question of returning to the restrictions of the policy of excluding others.

The costs of establishment, for the metropolis, would be minimal and the administrative expenses non-existent. For it was important that the colonies be left the greatest autonomy and be able to foresee their independence, the day when they would become "adult.". . .

In rereading this large book, this book of a young man in which the doctrine is hard to disengage from overly abundant compilation, one discerns a begging of the question of the necessity for colonial expansion. A reader who does not think of the "restoration of the wounded France" could, in effect, approve the thesis of Leroy-Beaulieu without inferring any obligation to create colonies. Since it was not a question of re-establishing monopolies or exclusive restrictions, why not develop trade, invest capital, furnish cadres of technicians to new countries without preliminary political conquest? But the necessity for prestige was not disputed at this epoch. Other publicists, like the Abbé Rabois-son, author of *Des Etudes sur les colonies et la colonisation au regard de la France* (1877) pointed out: "There has never been great power without great colonies. The apogee of the grandeur of empires always coincides with the height of their colonial expansion, their decadence with the loss of their colonies."

Gabriel Charmes wrote in *Le Journal des Débats* of October 19, 1880: "We must not forget that France has other frontiers besides the Vosges and that events could happen in the Mediterranean which would do her more harm than those which took place in Alsace-Lorraine."

.   .   .   .

Besides these writers one must undoubtedly make a place for the engineers whom the success of Lesseps [2] had filled with emulation. Roudaire developed his project for creation of an inland sea, uniting the Chads of the south of Tunisia and of Algeria with the Mediterranean, in the *Revue des deux Mondes* as early as 1874, and Duponchel defended his project for a trans-Sahara railroad before the Geographic Society of Lyons, as early as 1876. These engineers were able to invoke the necessity for political controls capable of ensuring order in the regions where such great works were to be undertaken. But one could

[2] Ferdinand de Lesseps (1805–1894): diplomat and engineer of the Suez Canal, which was opened in 1869. [Editor's note.]

reply to them that the Suez Canal was cut without the preliminary conquest of Egypt.

Thus the French, whose specific characteristic before 1870 had without doubt been liberalism, had become nationalists as well. Their literature abundantly demonstrates this fact as do the works of the historians of the period and an examination of the school-books. In the field of geography, this nationalism led to the elaboration of genuine colonial imperialism. The latter drew freely on economic arguments. But, among the men who referred to them, representatives of industry or commerce were the exception.

JULES FERRY: IMPERIAL ACTIVIST *

Thomas F. Power, Jr.

When Jules Ferry (1832–93) became prime minister in 1880, France's colonial possessions were widely regarded as unwanted children. Public indifference to their fate and resentment over the costs of their upkeep characterized the period. By 1885, however, the French overseas empire had grown from one to three million square miles— making it second in size only to the British empire. Ironically, the man most responsible for this transformation, Jules Ferry, who was twice premier (1880–81, 1883–85), fell from office on the issue of imperial expansion through the machinations of his political opponents. If the Third Republic repudiated Ferry, it warmly embraced the empire he had helped to build. Only later did Frenchmen come to appreciate his contributions to the gloire of their country. The following short summary of Ferry's commitment to empire is taken from Jules Ferry and the Renaissance of French Imperialism, written by Thomas F. Power, Jr., who is currently serving with the United Nations Technical Assistance Board in Pakistan.

Revival of the competition for empire was one of the most striking phenomena of the last quarter of the nineteenth century, for, following a period of disinterestedness in overseas possessions, the major powers

* Reprinted from *Jules Ferry and the Renaissance of French Imperialism* (New York: 1944), pp. 194–99, with omissions, by permission of Columbia University Press and the author. Copyright, 1944, by Columbia University Press.

raced to appropriate most of Africa, large parts of Asia and the islands in the Pacific and Indian oceans. A movement driven by intertwined nationalistic, economic and religious impulses with the first-named usually the most important, it gave France a huge overseas empire of which Jules Ferry was the chief harvester.

French expansion in the 1870's was unobtrusively begun by colonial officials without the knowledge of, or with only grudging approval from, Paris. They were predominantly naval and military men who practiced their art of war on relatively backward kingdoms and tribes for the love of *la patrie* and of adventure. Often they were encouraged and abetted by French colonists like those in Réunion, Algeria and Tunis. New oriental and tropical lands were opened up by merchant-adventurers like Dupuis in Tonkin and adventurous explorers like Brazza in Equatorial Africa. Little encouragement from the motherland was given these lonely imperialists for many years.

The leaders of France were for a decade much too busy to devote their energies to the empire. They had to repair the French economy after a war and revolution, rebuild the state with a new constitution achieved only after long struggles. The Republicans had first to secure political and then administrative and institutional control of the Third Republic. Moreover, France had no formal ally although she enjoyed the friendship of England. Bitter after defeat, she could not risk any serious involvements abroad.

Jules Ferry as a young man had no interest in colonial expansion. He was deeply concerned with domestic problems, his liberal faith was opposed to imperialism. He thought in European terms and was chiefly concerned with opposing the undemocratic Napoleonic Empire [1852–70]. Typical of the majority of Republicans, he was absorbed in domestic problems during the early years of the Republic and well into his first term as Premier of France. He had no plans for overseas expansion when he came into office and only after his sweeping educational reforms were nearly completed did he become interested in these questions. He was persuaded to embark on his first colonial venture by career diplomats and colleagues, alarmed at Italian ambitions in Tunisia, who proposed to preserve French prestige and guard Algeria by seizing the Regency. Ferry's predecessors had already secured the consent of England and Germany.[1]

---

[1] At the Berlin Congress of 1878, which gave France a free hand in Tunis. Confronted with Italian designs in that area and with Tunisian raids on French-governed Algeria, Ferry invaded Tunis. The Bey of Tunis capitulated and accepted a French protectorate (1881). [Editor's note.]

Once he was persuaded to act in Tunisia, Ferry launched into a many-pronged imperialistic drive, renewing French projects in Indo-China, Oceania and West Africa. Pronounced vigor in the colonial sphere characterized the balance of his years as Premier. Not only did he subsidize exploration of Africa and Asia as he had early done, but he undertook aggressive actions without properly informing Parliament of his intentions. He never had any long-range plan, but he moved opportunistically whenever a chance presented itself. If he thought he could easily add to the French domain, he moved in as he did in Annam and Madagascar. His formula was to subsidize, seize and suppress abroad and then to explain his actions at home. But he was seldom the initiator: his ability lay in perceiving a promising, even though precarious French foothold, organizing a campaign to secure it, doggedly hanging on, and exploiting all opportunities while holding a firm majority in Parliament. The only colony that was entirely his creation, from early exploration to final international ratification of French ownership, was Equatorial Africa, an outgrowth of Brazza's Congo discoveries. In each other field he was the heir of previous French occupation or ambition. His acquisitions included: Tunisia, the Congo, part of the French Sudan, Annam and Tonkin, several Pacific island archipelagos, and part of French Somaliland. He came close to securing Madagascar and the base he established there was later successfully enlarged, as indeed were most of his territorial gains. He nurtured French interests in the financial management of Egypt and instigated the establishment there of multiple European control, a beginning that was never carried through. He beat off diplomatic or military attacks on his conquests, by England, China, Belgium, Turkey and Italy. However, he probably dissipated his energies dangerously in attempting to take so many new colonies. Undoubtedly it was a source of weakness for him to have his energies spread so far over the globe.

Very important in persuading him to undertake several of his colonial expeditions were high civil servants, professional diplomats and military men. During his second term he needed little of this encouragement, and they merely bolstered his resolve. For the most part they were concerned about French prestige or diplomatic position. As Courcel [2] joined Barthélemy Saint-Hilaire [3] and tipped the balance in

[2] Alphonse, Baron de Courcel (1835–1919): director of political affairs at Ministry of Foreign Affairs (1880); ambassador to Berlin (1881); represented France at Berlin Congo Conference (1884); ambassador to London (1894–98). [Editor's note.]

[3] Jules Barthélemy Saint-Hilaire (1805–95): journalist, politician, man of letters; Minister of Foreign Affairs (1880–81). [Editor's note.]

the case of Tunisia, so Billot,[4] his successor at the Quai d'Orsay, was a chief advisor and goader in the case of Indo-China. The explorer Brazza fired Ferry's imagination for African expansion; Mahy, a deputy from Réunion, misled him into the Madagascar expedition. . . .

The aggressive imperial policy which Jules Ferry pursued would perhaps not have been possible and certainly would have been more hazardous had it not been for the support of Bismarck. The German Chancellor deliberately encouraged France to build an empire in order to distract her from the lost provinces. During 1884, Bismarck backed French imperial ambitions to use them as a weapon against England. Ferry was well aware of the reasons for Bismarck's support, which the Chancellor was fairly frank to admit. He refused to be pushed by the German statesman beyond the limits he set for himself, however. The Chancellor did not succeed in involving Ferry in any expedition or diplomatic move that did not suit his intentions. This Franco-German working agreement, a specific and limited entente, was the only co-operation of its sort between 1870 and 1914, and Jules Ferry certainly secured more concrete and lasting results therefrom than Germany. It was most useful to him in the West Africa, Indo-China and Madagascar questions, as well as in Egypt. Thanks to it, the European diplomatic ring was kept clear. Ferry could send his troops off without fear of threats or reprisals at home from hostile powers or coalitions. England was unable to protest, as she would often have liked to do, for fear of a continental alliance of secondary naval powers against her. Much of this situation was purely fortuitous for Jules Ferry. He could not possibly have engineered the Anglo-German coolness, for example—but he drew from it all the advantage possible. There must, however, be counted among the lasting results of Ferry's international policy the fact that an Anglo-French estrangement, which began shortly after the military intervention of England in Egypt, was made worse and persisted for nearly two decades. Moreover, loss of the race for Tunisia was a factor in influencing Italy to ally herself with Germany and Austria.

It has been often assumed that Ferry and his colleagues were primarily interested in acquiring new markets for French industry, new fields for French investors; or in protecting French commerce or finance when it was threatened by unsympathetic natives or the vicissitudes of the Great Depression. Such was not the case. Economic factors alone

---

[4] Albert Billot (1841–1922): diplomat, historian, political economist; as Councillor of State at Ministry of Foreign Affairs helped to promote the conquest of Tonkin; ambassador to Portugal and later Italy (1890–98). [Editor's note.]

or predominantly were hardly ever responsible for the initiation of French colonial policy. The total French exports to the colonies which were acquired during Ferry's time constituted but an infinitesimal fraction of the nation's trade; French investments were small except in Egypt where France had long been supporting her bondholders. Egypt was a special case for there was no thought or hope of making it a French colony. Jules Ferry was first determined to continue to protect the bondholders because he thought this a proper function for government. In his second Ministry he added to that continuing concern a desire to regain a share in the political as well as financial control of Egypt. Elsewhere, there were French investments only in Tunisia, and on those the bondholders were having no difficulty in collecting their usurious returns when Ferry took over. Nor was there an immediate rush of French trade, private construction of utilities or investment in the newly acquired colonies. Conspicuously lacking from Ferry's creed was a demand for raw materials. Only later did imports of tropical and mineral products bulk large in French interest. In the early days of expansion the Great Depression had not yet hit France heavily, and French commerce was but slightly affected by the rising world tariff barriers. When Ferry's expansion was *in medias res,* depression conditions were setting in and he did not hesitate, on the floor of Parliament, to use the threat of rising European and American tariffs to justify his acquisition of new markets. In any case, Ferry, as a good bourgeois, strong nationalist, and good politician, would not naturally oppose measures presumably to improve his country's prosperity. But his early expansion bore only slight reference to potential markets. More often than not, economic factors were only the tools of diplomacy or parliamentary controversy.

There is no evidence of pressure or influence exerted on Ferry or his colleagues by organized pressure groups, important trading associations, manufacturers, or investment houses in metropolitan France. Doubtless some individuals like Dupuis encouraged him to push on but there were no scandalous deals and no personal peculation in this French imperialism. What economic pressure there was came mostly from French colonists. It is true that during the period there was greatly increased industrial activity and a wealth of new products that generally stimulated trade and industry, but such products did not flow in great streams to the lands over which Ferry extended his control. There were few instances where threats to marketing by hostile natives furnished a motive for expansion.

When Ferry embarked on his colonial schemes, there was no organized colonial propaganda movement. Only a few publicists and academic writers without following called for an empire. Colonial societies and their periodicals were rapidly appearing, but their weight was felt only in the succeeding decade. Popular interest in the French empire was only slowly aroused until imaginations were fired by tales of natural and archeological wonders in mysterious Africa and Asia. National pride was inflated by the prestige of owning such mysterious and reputedly wealthy lands. The saga of Brazza aroused great public enthusiasm and interest in the race for Equatorial Africa, but such feeling was not evidenced for the other territories into which Ferry sent troops. Indeed, had Jules Ferry possessed a warmer personality, a greater flair for publicity to popularize his acquisitions, he might have experienced less criticism. As it was, he drove determinedly and aggressively forward but without attempting to capture public interest, presenting France with conquests, but not with inspiring panoramas of imperial splendor.

The opposition to Ferry's program of colonial expansion has been generally overrated and misunderstood, owing to the fact that his loss of the Premiership apparently came twice as a result of his policy in Tunisia and Tonkin. Actually both defeats were accounted for chiefly by growing parliamentary dislike of Ferry's domestic program. Parliament, like the public, was not pleased by the cost in men and money of the expeditions to Tunisia, Madagascar and Indo-China, but it supported Ferry until it tired of his domestic policies and found a convenient excuse to turn him out of office in a seemingly disastrous military reverse in Indo-China.[5] Parliament made a point of retaining the new possessions, even though it defeated the man responsible for their acquisition. On measures dealing with colonial expansion Ferry secured substantially as much support as on domestic matters, and his majorities in both cases declined together. The Radicals who disliked his moderate reforms, his domineering personality and firm management of governmental affairs, fought as bitterly on colonial as they did on domestic questions. The Conservatives, as a group, opposed most of his colonial expeditions. They supported only the Madagascar enterprise, although some few of their more nationalistic members supported all expansion.

That is not to say that all the opposition to imperialism was entirely hypocritical. Many extremely nationalistic *revanchards* were thoroughly

[5] The defeat of French troops at Lang-Son led to Ferry's resignation on 30 March 1885. [Editor's note.]

convinced that all French energy should be devoted to preparing to strike back at Germany and recover Alsace and Lorraine. A few Radicals were pacifists on intellectual grounds, staunch supporters of the doctrines of the fraternity of mankind and opposed to all imperialism. But for the most part, Ferry was faced with an intransigent coalition of Right and Left.

The need to secure appropriations from Parliament forced Ferry to formulate a rationale of expansion *ex post facto*. On the forge of parliamentary debate, this took its shape of economic imperialism. His early explanations and justifications were principally devoted to arguments of prestige and national honor. But late in 1883 the economic arguments came to the fore, and in retirement Ferry cultivated them to full flower. Those who have read only his later explanations of policy have been misled to believe that they were characteristic of his whole imperialistic career. That this is not true may be most strikingly seen in contrasting the debates on Tunisia and Tonkin. The economic arguments advanced in the latter case were useful to win over a Parliament disposed to a tender regard for business interests. Especially this was the case when economic distress set in late in Ferry's second Ministry. Doubtless he was then really interested in opening markets, for a great race for colonies in Africa and Asia was developing, and he was faced with rivalry on every side.

Ferry also professed to champion a civilizing mission and duty that compelled France to bring the beauties and truths of French culture and Christianity to the backward peoples and free them from such barbaric practices as slavery. This argument was useful to the prosaic Ferry who believed in the power of education, but was hardly a mainspring of action. Directly bound with considerations of prestige was the necessity of global strategy for an imperial and maritime power. For that reason Ferry acquired naval bases useful both for the merchant marine and warships.

Whatever the means and motives, the policy of Ferry did endow France with a great empire. A few years later one of his young assistants, Gabriel Hanotaux,[6] as Foreign Minister, as well as a succession of French generals and explorers extended the boundaries of the possessions Ferry had harvested for France. This empire, for all its shortcomings, made the Third Republic a major world power.

[6] (1853–1944): historian and statesman; Minister of Foreign Affairs (1894–95, 1896–98); author of many historical works including a study of French colonial expansion with Alfred Martineau (Paris: 1930–33). [Editor's note.]

COMMERCIAL AND COLONIAL POLICIES
OF IMPERIAL GERMANY *

Mary E. Townsend

Mary E. Townsend, who is Professor Emeritus of European History at Teachers College, Columbia University, has written extensively about German colonial expansion in the late nineteenth century. Her two principal works in this field, Origins of Modern German Colonialism, 1871–1885 (New York: 1921) and The Rise and Fall of Germany's Colonial Empire, 1884–1918 (New York: 1930) are still used as standard references and provide numerous insights into the official and unofficial forces that combined to move Germany into the competition for colonies. In her more recent account of German expansion overseas, which follows below, Professor Townsend goes further than her earlier works would suggest in stressing the role of commercial interests in the acquisition and administration of territories in Africa and elsewhere. However, for whatever reasons acquired, the German Empire was short-lived. With the outbreak of World War I the Germans were the first of the new imperial powers to experience the loss of their overseas empire. No sooner had fighting begun than the Japanese seized the Caroline, Mariana, and Marshall Islands; Australia occupied German New Guinea; and New Zealand captured Western Samoa. Germany's possessions in Africa were similarly expropriated by the Allied Powers, and after the war they were parceled out as trusts or mandates under League of Nations auspices. Britain and France divided the Cameroons and Togoland between them; German East Africa was carved up among the British (Tanganyika), the Belgians (Ruanda-Urundi), and the Portuguese (part of Mozambique). The Union of South Africa retained control over German South-west Africa and the remaining dependencies of the defeated country became mandates of the occupying powers. Almost overnight Imperial Germany had shriveled to a mundane republic shorn of its overseas empire.

* Reprinted from "The Economic Impact of Imperial Germany," *The Tasks of Economic History* (supplemental issue of *The Journal of Economic History*, December, 1943), 124–34 with omissions, by permission of the editors of *The Journal of Economic History*.

I

When Hitler based so much of his campaign of 1936–1937 for the return of the colonies upon the Fatherland's economic need of them, he was reverting to the pattern of Germany's colonial history. It mattered not that the economic value of these colonies had been proven negligible or, at least, problematical so far as any advantage in trade and raw materials accruing to the empire was concerned. He and the Nazi leaders continued to stress the economic motive of expansion and aggression; to emphasize the close connection between commercial and colonial policies which had always characterized German imperialism.

This predominant role played by the trader in the acquisition, establishment, and administration of the German colonies placed him in a unique position of influence in the economic life of the empire. From the beginning, he effected an identity of colonial and commercial interests; a union of economic forces which also coincided with the rising power of the capitalist in political life. Such an irresistible combination could not fail to contribute substantially to an intense German economic nationalism which demanded a policy of aggressive expansion both in trade and overseas empire. That this ultimately led to disaster in its impact upon the economic life of Western Europe, the first quarter of the twentieth century made all too evident. Fully to realize the strength of this union of commercial and colonial interests and hence identity of policies, it is essential briefly to review some of the circumstances of its origin before indicating its more important results.

In the first place, wherever one looks at the various parts of the former German colonial empire, he will observe that the trader was always the effective colonial pioneer. The Hanseatic towns, indeed, in line with their old tradition, provided the largest number of actors for the commercial drama that was to form the first part of the great cycle of German colonial activities.[1] Southwest Africa owed its existence to F. E. Lüderitz, head of the important mercantile house in Bremen, long interested in trade in Africa; East Africa's acquisition was built upon established foundations laid down by early trading firms, especially the Hamburg House of O'Swald, where, even in 1874, German export trade

[1] The Hanseatic League originated in the thirteenth century as an association of north German commercial centers and played a major role in the economic development of Northern Europe. Dominated by Lübeck, Hamburg, and Bremen, this loose confederation of over seventy towns established factories or "counters" in Bruges, London, and other cities and secured important trading concessions for its members. [Editor's note.]

from Zanzibar amounted to three times more than the British; Togoland and Cameroons were the result of the lively activities of several Hamburg and Bremen mercantile houses, chief of which was the celebrated House of Woermann which secured a commercial grip upon the entire district and whose packet boats carried on a regular trade with all the West African coast.

In the South Seas, also, merchants of the Hanse towns were the pioneers. The famous Hamburg House of Godeffroy, with its head-quarters at Samoa, controlled trading stations all over the South Seas, organizing a vast trade in copra and winning from the British the title of the "South Sea King"; while the firms of Hernsheim and Robertson, active in New Britain, the Caroline and Marshall Islands, were but forerunners of many powerful business houses trafficking in the South Pacific. All of these commercial interests formed the beginnings of Kai-serwilhelmsland and the Bismarck Archipelago.

Likewise, in the Near East, commercial interests were paramount in originating what became the *Drang nach Osten*.[2] As early as 1872, von Pressel, an eminent German railway engineer, was retained by the Sul-tan to develop plans for railways in Turkey, in which project the Deutsche Bank and the Württemsbergische Bank immediately became interested. This encouraged the merchants already competing with Brit-ish and French interests, with the result that Germany's economic ex-pansion into the Near East between 1888–1900 formed one of the wonders wrought by her industrial revolution. For, by 1900, German commercial groups were by far the most active in Constantinople and in Asia Minor; whereas, in 1888, Great Britain and France had prac-tically monopolized Turkey's trade and finance.

Besides their work as pioneers in every part of Germany's colonial empire, the commercial interests formed the only effective force in inaugurating the colonial movement at home. These merchants suc-ceeded in persuading Bismarck to adopt an official colonial policy. Deaf to the intellectual arguments and propaganda of political economists, scientists, historians, that "professor-led multitude," as well as to the im-portunities of explorers and missionaries, the Iron Chancellor finally succumbed to the economic pressure applied by the commercial colonial-ists. For their demands for an official colonial policy were based not upon an abstract theory or cult but upon the more practical founda-tion of actual achievement, at once substantial and obvious. Colonial

[2] Literally, "desire" or "push" towards the East, thus "eastward expansion." [Editor's note.]

expansion at the hands of the commercial interests had become an accomplished fact; it had created a situation fraught with nationalistic competition with which the government was obliged to reckon.

Even from the time of the treaty of Frankfort,[3] the commercial interests had clamoured for official colonialism: a Bremen group of thirty-five firms demanded France's surrender of the port of Saigon in China as a base to protect German shipowners and merchants; while Hamburg traders asked for Cochin China, Martinique, St. Pierre, and Miquelon as spoils of the peace. Continuing throughout the seventies and early eighties, the petitions from commercial interests for government protection became legion as their ventures overseas kept pace with Germany's rapidly developing economic life. In the South Seas and in Africa, competitive clashes between German and British commercial interests led to sharp exchanges between foreign offices which underlined the need for an official colonial policy and strengthened the commercial-colonial tie.

Coincident with this pressure from outside upon the government, the commercial colonialists built up an internal colonial movement at home. Their instruments here consisted of a wide propaganda, the creation of the Kolonialverein, the winning of political influence for the colonial party, and the exertion of special economic pressure upon the government. With what success their efforts were finally crowned, Bismarck's telegram to Lüderitz of April 24, 1884, officially proclaiming his settlements in Southwest Africa under the protection of the government, is witness. The German colonial empire was launched and the commercial interests had been its chief engineers.

II

One of the most important and far-reaching results of the dominance of the commercial interests in the origins of German colonialism was the position they won at the outset in colonial administration. Bismarck's original plan of delegating to colonial companies all responsibility for the colonies constituted, indeed, a proof of the paramount position of the traders. He wished to designate these colonial societies, in the form of chartered companies, the sole agents of his new imperial policy. To them he planned to surrender all the duties of administration, taxation, land development, and negotiations with the native peo-

[3] Bismarck's "dictated peace" formally ending the Franco-Prussian war on 10 May 1871. [Editor's note.]

ples. There was to be no colonial bureaucracy, no colonial military forces functioning under the central government; the empire was to interfere only when it became necessary to exercise protection from the other powers. Thus the title for Germany's overseas possessions became the *Schutzgebiete*,[4] not the "Colonies." For the Chancellor regarded these protectorates primarily as a "business proposition"; his slogans were: "The flag follows trade," and "First the trader, then the soldier."

To be sure, this plan failed of success mainly because the seventeenth-century system of great colonial societies enjoying sovereign or nearly sovereign rights was out of harmony with the nineteenth-century conditions. The existence of strong national and economically competitive states prevented the companies from occupying a sufficiently important position. Also, these latter lacked financial resources, national support, and prestige and consequently were unable adequately to develop the colonial resources, to control the native populations, or to cope with foreign complications. Hence the central government, often at the instigation of the traders themselves, who realized their need for protection, was obliged to assume direct rule over the colonies.

Even though the privileged sovereign societies disappeared, as such, and never were able to assume the responsibility of colonial administration which Bismarck designed for them, they resolved into commercial companies which maintained the grip of the trader upon affairs in the colonies themselves. For they perpetuated and multiplied the land grants, the mining and plantation rights, the extension of all kinds of concessions. Serving as a screen to national expansion, they also considerably extended the colonial territory. It was, indeed, the unchecked control of these commercial companies which led to the colonial "Scandals" of exploitation, ill-treatment of natives, monopolistic graft and corruption, and brought down upon them the severe indictment of the Socialists and other opponents of the colonial policy. The very strength and severity of the indictment was proof of the extraordinary powers of the companies and their commercial interests.

Nor did the failure of Bismarck's plan and the investing of his colonial administration in the imperial government decrease the influence of the trader therein, at home; he merely transferred his control to those official agencies set up to administer the colonies. This was not difficult because, since 1876, the commercial interest had come to enjoy an ever-increasing confidence and co-operation with the Chancellor. Bismarck, indeed, after the first "foundation years" of the new empire, became

4 "The Protectorates." [Editor's note.]

hand in glove with the merchants and traders and with their agents, the bankers. More and more were they included in the inner councils of government, more and more were their wishes and interests considered, their demands met. The Chancellor's vigorous policy of protecting imperial trade overseas, as witnessed by the negotiation of the Tongan, Samoan, and other trade treaties during the late seventies, and his strong support accorded the Samoan Subsidy Bill in 1879, designed to rescue the German trading interests in the South Seas, which were seriously threatened by the financial failure of the famous House of Godeffroy, had all resulted in a close entente between the government and the traders.

Continually, also, Bismarck referred to this group for advice and help and, as we shall later observe, for political support. . . . It was only logical, therefore, that when the Chancellor was obliged to create a central, colonial administration, the commercial interests should be strongly represented. Thus, their influence was especially felt in the Kolonialrat or Colonial Council, created in 1890 as an advisory council to the colonial section of the Foreign Office. The Chancellor nominated its members from a list which he invited the colonial companies and all those individuals who had important interests overseas to submit. It is significant that of the nineteen originally named, twelve members represented the mercantile firms doing business in the colonies. When the central administration was reformed in 1907 and the colonial office transformed into a separate department of state with a Secretary of Colonies at its head, the Kolonialrat was abolished but it was superseded by a permanent commission for the economic affairs of the colonies; here, again, its membership, which finally reached twenty-five, was drawn from the chambers of commerce of such cities as Hamburg, Bremen, Cologne, Mannheim, Chemnitz.

Also indicative of the influence of the commercial interests in the central administration was the character of the first Colonial Secretary, Bernhard Dernburg.[5] First and foremost a man of business "in whose Jewish veins ran the spirit of finance," his past experience as a banker prepared him to understand and to promote the interests of the commercial group, to trust the trader rather than the administrator. First and foremost in his plans was the economic development of the colonies. He thoroughly believed in the undisputed value of colonies to the home country as a solution for the problems of marketing surplus goods and of providing raw materials. His idea was, on the one hand, to pro-

[5] (1865–1937): Secretary of Colonies (1907–10); Minister of Finance (1919–20. [Editor's note.]

duce in the colonies those commodities, foodstuffs, and raw materials which Germany was obliged to import from other nations; and, on the other, so to civilise the natives that in time they would be consuming quantities of clocks, toys, leather purses, and automobile tires all emblazoned with the trade-mark, "Made in Germany."

Most of Secretary Dernburg's policies, such as his railroad program in Africa, his colonial research institutes with their work for better agriculture, stock-raising, and disease-prevention, or his colonial schools for training "experts" in administration and colonial development, combined to advance the interests of trade in the colonies, which began to exhibit a more satisfactory increase. Moreover, his successors in office, Dr. Lindquist and Dr. Solf, continued his high-pressure methods of stimulating the development of the colonies, thereby aggravating keen competition with other nations and emphasizing economic nationalism.

Besides these official and direct channels of influence in the central colonial administration enjoyed by the commercial interests, there existed other indirect and extra-legal means through which they exercised their power. Chief of these was the very influential Kolonialverein or Colonial Society and the Kolonialwirtschaftliches Kommittee or Economic Committee, the economic section of the Colonial Society after 1902. Prominent in their origins, commercial interests always maintained extraordinary control in these agencies of colonial propaganda, research, exploitation, education, and political action. The Economic Committee, indeed, was founded by a group, who, deploring the government's inactivity in colonial development, formed a Committee for the Importation of Products from German Colonies. . . .

As a result, the contents of these commercial-colonial agencies with the imperial government and with public opinion were constant and effective. Generally speaking, it may be said that the Kolonialverein concentrated before 1907 upon securing and shaping a central, colonial administration with all its appurtenances; and after 1907, threw its efforts into the work of the Economic Committee to develop the colonies. Among the successful policies which it promoted, thereby identifying itself more closely with those in power were: the establishment of an independent colonial ministry; the construction of a well-articulated, central, administrative machine with all its details of courts and councils; the support of local reforms within the colonies, and of all those measures, such as training schools, research institutes, the study of tropical diseases, and the education of the natives—in short, the new "Scientific Colonialism," designed to enhance their economic value.

Furthermore, the Kolonialverein and the other organizations of colonial and commercial interests lent vigorous aid to those corollaries of their own policies, as symbolized by the Navy League and the Pan-German League, which coincided with the *Weltpolitik* of the imperial government, thus welding a closer bond between them.

III

In so far as this brief discussion admits, the identity of commercial and colonial interests and the influence which they came to wield in the government has been sufficiently established, perhaps, to explain their dominant position in the economic life of Germany and consequently in her relations with the other nations of Western Europe. Two examples, however, of their specific policies, the impact of which upon Western Europe was signally momentous, will serve to illustrate the extent of their influence. The first one concerns the inauguration of a protective tariff and the return to a neomercantilism the repercussions of which in Europe were especially contributory to economic nationalism.

There can hardly be any doubt that the commercial colonialists not only formed a determining influence in Bismarck's desertion of free trade and his adoption of a protective tariff, but that they fixed this system upon Germany's economy by their political machinations and manipulations. Their efforts to force the government to extend its protection over their well-founded trade establishments overseas, in Africa and in the South Seas, as evidenced by the long list of their petitions to Bismarck from 1871 on, had concretely demonstrated to the Chancellor the utter futility of his dependence upon free trade, as well as the inseparable connection of trade protection and political prestige. Before 1874, Bismarck had trusted to a liberal trade policy to open all countries and colonies to Germany; and this had worked fairly well so long as Gladstone managed British affairs. But after 1874, the doctrines of the Manchester School began to seem more ideal than practical; with the progress of industry and shipping and the increase of population an imperialistic tendency took possession of every nation. Great Britain, for instance, annexed the Fiji Islands in the South Seas in 1874, dispossessed the German traders and evicted them from their lands and buildings without indemnity; British and American claims on Samoa likewise conflicted with those of the German merchants; and Spain began to take measures to hamper German trade and possible settlement in the Spanish colonial possessions. In short the "dream of equal opportunity" in overseas trade was being rudely and finally dispelled and it was the activities of these commercial colonialists that were demonstrating the situation. They were the first group to grasp the significance of changed conditions, to prove that equality of economic opportunity existed nowhere for Germany, to elicit from the government the series of South Seas treaties of trade, amity, and protection. From these it was but a logical step to a thorough-going adoption of a national protective tariff in 1879.

Moreover, this commercial, colonial group, which had so directly contributed to Bismarck's new fiscal policy, provided the government with the political support which it so sorely needed for protectionism in the Reichstag. Inevitably, Bismarck had alienated his old, powerful friends, the National Liberals, upon whom he had relied since 1871, by his repudiation of free trade. A split in the party ensued and those members of the left wing who clung to traditional, liberal ideas deserted the government and joined the ranks of the opposition. To counterbalance their loss, the commercial colonists seized the opportunity to rally to Bismarck's support. Many of them belonged to the National Liberal party, not to the old group, which was becoming more national than liberal. These new Liberals, like the Hamburg and Bremen merchants, Woermann and Godeffroy, came to represent, indeed, the modern type of National Liberals in Germany who broke with the real liberalism which accepted the free-trade principles of the Hanse towns.

And, in the early eighties, Bismarck was especially disposed to welcome these adherents to his fiscal policy both to combat the attacks of the opposition and to fill up the ranks of his allies depleted by the defection of the left wing of the National Liberals. For the Hanse towns were opposed to protection. Hamburg, Bremen, and Lübeck preferred, for the most part, to preserve their old tradition of free trade, which they found more profitable, and hence they constituted the strongest forces of the opposition. But the firm of Godeffroy, by far the most influential firm both in Hamburg and in colonial activities in the South Seas, stood firmly for protection, largely because of its overseas interests and its inevitable clashes with the commercial ambitions of other powers. It had endeavored to make Hamburg enter the Zollverein. The same situation likewise prevailed in Bremen where the firm of Mosle and Company, equally influential in the colonial policy, strongly advocated protection against the majority opinion of the city. Naturally, Bismarck heartily accepted the support afforded by these two powerful firms situated in the two enemy camps; it proved invaluable in his determined effort to establish protectionism as a national policy.

IV

Finally, a second conspicuous policy employed by the commercial colonialists which had a serious impact upon Europe was their ruthless suppression of all political and organized opposition to expansion by the clever device of raising it to a national and patriotic issue. This policy was especially significant because it is doubtful whether any colonial power had as much parliamentary opposition to economic imperialism as Germany encountered in the Reichstag. Had it been permitted to prevail, who can estimate its influence as a curb upon national competition and antagonism?

Leaders of the opposition were the Social Democrats ably assisted by part of the Catholic Center, and often by the Radicals. Socialist objections were founded upon their own creed well summed up by Franz Mehring [6]: "Colonies are merely trading stations. The capitalist system plays the rôle of capital accumulation. It enriches the shipping trade and assures a world market." . . . To these anti-imperialist arguments, the Catholics added their condemnation of the sins of robbery, cruelty, and murder in the treatment of the natives. Altogether the opposition's indictment of the whole system of commercial colonialism affords a confirmation of the identity of colonial and commercial interests and their extraordinary power.

When the opposition in the Reichstag became vocal, as it generally did in debates over the budgets which revealed the great costs of the colonies, it was consistently met by aspersions upon its patriotism and failure to support the "national honor." . . . To destroy the opposition and to save the program, a veritable fire of chauvinistic patriotism was prepared, lighted, and kept alive. National animosity against Great Britain was deliberately stimulated and the opposition was branded with the crime of attempting to control the foreign policy contrary to to the maintenance of national honor.

This policy was applied again and again whenever the opponents of

[6] (1846–1919): Socialist politician and historian; opposed war in 1914; later joined the Leninist revolutionary movement known as the Spartacists, whose leaders were shot during the abortive uprising of January, 1919. [Editor's note.]

economic imperialism disputed the budgets. But its climax was reached in the parliamentary crisis of 1906–1907 when the opposition succeeded in causing the rejection of the supplementary estimate to maintain in Southwest Africa the expeditionary force engaged in quelling a native insurrection. As a result the Reichstag was dissolved and the ensuing electoral campaign became a tug of war between the protagonists of colonial and commercial expansion and the anti-expansionists. During the debates preceding dissolution a veritable flood of criticisms, condemnatory disclosures, and convicting evidence of all the evils of economic imperialism was unloosed. Never in any parliamentary assembly had such an indictment of colonial and commercial expansion taken place; and during the election campaign this was transferred to the propagandistic speeches and press of the opposition.

From the outset, however, the issue was squarely defined as one of world policy: "Germany's position in the world is menaced. The forthcoming election will decide whether Germany is capable of developing into a world power from a European power," challenged the *Norddeutsche Allgemeine Zeitung*, indicating the unprecedented entrance of the government as leader of the campaign. The dissolved Reichstag was labeled "unpatriotic" and the minor appropriation for Southwest Africa was magnified into an issue of Germany's whole imperialistic and national future. The Radical People's Party, a former enemy of expansion and of the protective tariff, deserted the opposition because the Chancellor directly appealed to it for support on patriotic grounds. All the nationalistic and patriotic societies such as the Navy League, the Pan-German League, and the Association for the Suppression of Socialism rallied to the support of the expansionists. Admirably equipped to disseminate appeals to "patriotism," they gloried in a campaign "for the honor of German arms; for the retention of the colonies; for the protection of Germany's prestige in the world."

As a result of this intense nationalizing of the issue, the opposition was defeated mainly at the expense of the Social Democrats, and the pro-expansionist forces won a resounding victory. As the *Norddeutsche Allgemeine Zeitung* boasted the day after the election: "The German people, when national questions are involved, can ride down everything that stands in the way of the nation. They will not tolerate the slightest weakening of their national strength, even when only an African colony and a couple of thousand men are concerned. . . . The national, imperial and world political idea has won a brilliant victory among the German people."

THE NEW AFRICA BETWEEN
EAST AND WEST *

Margery Perham

Introduction †

Since 1945 the world has witnessed a remarkably sustained and successful effort on the part of colonial peoples to emancipate themselves from European domination. In this short period Great Britain, France, Belgium, and Italy have together relinquished control over the lives and fortunes of more than 886,000,000 individuals or almost one quarter of the world's population. In magnitude and complexity this process of decolonization has few precedents in history; and the scarcity of first-rate literature on this subject is some indication of the difficulties involved in sifting, refining, and then interpreting the mass of data—much of it inaccurate—concerned with this phenomenon. The student of the contraction of Europe in the twentieth century approaches the contemporary scene in Africa, Asia, India, and the Pacific with justifiable diffidence. He is hampered by the abundance of unreliable information and discouraged by the ease with which his most careful calculations are rendered invalid by the pressure of events. So numerous are the variables at work within the new or emergent nations that any general survey of decolonization is bound to be speculative if not obsolete by the time it has appeared in print. The search for the ingredients of stability or instability that lie beneath the surface of each society presents many difficulties, and yet it is only through such a quest that one can learn to distinguish between mirage and reality or revolution and evolution. Clues as to the prospects of the new nations are not to be found in the verbal pyrotechnics or voting habits of their representatives in the United Nations. Nor do the equivocal relationships of the former colonies with the superpowers of the East and West provide the observer with profound insights into the consequences of

---

* Reprinted from The Colonial Reckoning: The End of Imperial Rule in Africa in the Light of British Experience by Margery Perham, by permission of Alfred A Knopf, Inc., and Willis Kingsley Wing and William Collins Sons & Co. Ltd. Copyright, 1961, 1962, by Margery Perham.
† [Editor's introduction.]

decolonization. Instead one must look into each nation or ethnic unit for those signs, often intangible, that indicate how successfully the partial or complete vacuum created by the withdrawal of imperial power has been filled.

The prerequisites of political stability and economic viability vary from one country to another. But in almost every case it is patently absurd to expect the new nations to emulate democratic ideals and institutions which took the English-speaking peoples some 800 years, not to mention a number of civil wars and revolutions, to evolve. Political man, moreover, does not live by representative institutions alone. What really matters, as an English prime minister, Arthur Balfour, once remarked, is the will to make the system work. Without the existence of a consensus that government must go on, even the best political system is doomed. In some of the new nations there is a tendency to assume that the function of the opposition is to stop the machine: "Nothing easier of course," Balfour observed, "but hopeless."

The article which follows focuses these considerations in terms of global power politics. Since it does not describe how the new nations came into being—and we know of no convenient book or article which does—we shall here attempt a rapid summing up of the liquidation of empire to date. In the transformation of Western Europe's colonial empires to nationhood, only Portugal has managed to retain the major portion of her overseas possessions. India's forcible seizure of the three Portuguese enclaves of Goa, Damao, and Diu in 1961, however, and continued turbulence in Angola have shown that the days of Portugal's imperial rule are also numbered. In 1949 the Netherlands formally surrendered control of their East Indian possessions to the Republic of Indonesia, which later acquired Dutch New Guinea or West Irian (1963). At the end of 1951 Italy relinquished all claims over Libya, which became the first independent state created under United Nations auspices. A year later the former Italian colony of Eritrea was federated with Ethiopia; and in 1960 Somalia, an Italian United Nations trusteeship since 1950, became independent. In June, 1960 the Belgians recognized the independence of the Republic of the Congo, and two years later their United Nations trusteeship of Ruanda-Urundi ended in the creation of the Kingdom of Burundi and the Republic of Ruanda. By 1962 the only dependent remnants of the former German colonial empire in Africa were German South-west Africa administered as a province of South Africa and a portion of German East Africa awarded to Portugal in 1919 and absorbed by Mozambique.

The liquidation of empire has been far more striking in the case of

France and Great Britain, whose former colonies have usually received internal autonomy several years before clearing the final hurdle of independence. Beginning with their withdrawal from Cambodia and Laos in 1949, the French have granted independence, either voluntarily or after agonizing conflict, to the following countries: Vietnam (1955), Morocco and Tunisia (1956), Guinea, the Ivory Coast, and Senegal (1958), Cameroon, Chad, Togo, the Congo Republic, Dahomey, Mauritania, Niger, the Central African Republic, Gabon, Mali, Upper Volta, Malagasy (all in 1960), and Algeria (1962), while Pondicherry and other holdings in India were transferred to Indian control in 1962. With only a few exceptions these former colonies and protectorates have maintained close financial, technical, and economic ties with France whether as members of the French Union (1946), the French Community (1958), or not.

In the former British Empire the separation of colonial ties has involved a much larger population than in Overseas France but far less bloodshed. The roll call of independent states includes India and Pakistan (1947), Burma and Ceylon (1948), Sudan (1956), Ghana and Malaya (1957), Cyprus, Nigeria, and Somaliland (1960), Sierra Leone, Southern Cameroons, and Tanganyika (1961), Jamaica, Trinidad and Tobago, and Uganda (1962), North Borneo, Sarawak, Singapore, Kenya, and Zanzibar (1963). In the course of liquidating their empire the British have emancipated a population estimated at 662,000,000—a figure which includes two populous areas that have gained independence within the past year, Kenya with 7,287,000, and Malaysia (excluding Malaya) with 2,948,000. As of January, 1964, some 12,500,000 still remain under British colonial administration. Of the eighteen nations granted independence since 1945, thirteen have become members of the Commonwealth. In addition, New Zealand's United Nations trusteeship of Western Samoa, which was seized from the Germans in the First World War, formally terminated in 1962. Western Samoa—Eastern Samoa is a United States possession—thus became the first, and so far only, independent native state in the Pacific.

By 1963 only three of the eleven territories formerly under the United Nations International Trusteeship system were still dependencies: Australian New Guinea and Nauru, and the American-administered Marshall, Caroline, and Mariana Islands. Africa presents the most dramatic example of Europe's imperial disintegration. In 1945 only four countries—Egypt, Ethiopia, Liberia, and South Africa—were independent. Since that date thirty so-called nations have been carved out of the former empires, and several other colonies are moving *rapidly toward independence. In sum, the only phenomenon comparable in scale and significance to this abrogation of colonial ties was the original "scramble" for Africa, Asia, and the islands of the Pacific that took almost the same length of time.*

Outside the Soviet "empire" the work of liquidation proceeds at a steady pace. Old colonies become new nations; federations formed today dissolve tomorrow; in their search for security the "uncommitted" nations form hasty alliances that fragment in kaleidoscopic fashion. Suffering the throes of industrialization, deficient in trained technicians and professional personnel, hypersensitive to criticism, and alarmed by the forces of disunity, some of these new nations have resorted to autocratic rule and police-state methods. The rise of single-party systems and personality cults in Africa and elsewhere has shown that the transition to representative government and civil liberties will be as slow and as prone to coercion as was that to independence.

The following is taken from the published version of Miss Perham's Reith Lectures broadcast by the BBC in 1961. Miss Margery Perham has long been an authority on African affairs; she is now Senior Fellow of Nuffield College, Oxford.

. . . They [the new African states] have awoken into a strangely situated world which offers them a political compensation for their physical weakness. Because of the apparent equality of power between the free world and the Communist states, and because the nature of modern war is such that it is almost impossible to wage it, the so-called third, or uncommitted, world holds a balancing position out of all proportion to its military strength. This third world consists largely of ex-colonial states, and now the twenty-eight new African states come crowding in to join their older African neighbours, Ethiopia, Egypt, and Liberia. Eleven of these new states have less than three million inhabitants: some of them have only a million or less, but the vote of each counts as much as the vote of the United States, Russia, or Britain. Here is a fantastic discrepancy between legal status and real power. How serious are its results? Is there perhaps even some advantage in having a kind of detached, neutral jury who cast their votes according to their main objectives? These are to attack the remaining strongholds of colonialism; to ban war and, above all, the atomic weapons; and to induce the rich powers to direct to their own empty coffers the wealth they are pouring into armaments.

.   .   .   .

So long as the world's balance hangs so evenly, and has to be maintained, short of war, by rather misnamed diplomatic methods, then so long will the neutrals hold their make-weight power. The African states are certainly fortunate in the date of their birth as the very existence of UNO [the U.N.] offers them a great international auditorium where the smallest power can make a resounding speech to the world, and where the poorest power, which cannot afford much in the way of embassies, can conduct its foreign affairs in the lobbies.

But the more deeply we look into the world situation, the less able are we to be optimistic about the results of bringing this mass of small powers to birth. All states want to ban war—except when they can find no other way of achieving the ends nearest their interests or their safety. It already appears that in pursuit of their major aim the anti-colonialist states regard armed force, revolution, and even war as legitimate methods. So long as the world's nations cannot bring themselves to give the United Nations both the international principles and the power to achieve peaceful change, so long will states resort to national violence. The major Western powers have never been able, partly because of the great division in the world, to rely upon international action to protect their interests, and they have therefore had to shift their stance from power to law, as occasion seemed to demand, in a way that has laid them open to the accusation of inconsistency and even hypocrisy. It is therefore easy enough for the large company of small new states, who have their deep bias against Western domination, to condemn these powers. Few, indeed, of the world's nations have clean records. Britain, France, and America have all lately resorted to private war to try to protect their interests. The records of Germany and Italy over the last few decades hardly qualify them for moral leadership, and the Communist states could not even begin to compete for it. Yet the struggle for the difficult ideal of international law and action must go on if the world is not to slide into complete anarchy. It is therefore important that the Western powers should understand both the character and the strength of the anti-colonial passion which unites the majority of the world's states against them, those states which, because of their weakness and their needs, could be the keenest supporters of the United Nations. . . .

The young African states are at least learning that they are no more immune than the wicked old nations from the international evils of frontier disputes and irredentism, nor even from the ideological differences that have led to groups being called by the names of the different capitals in which they confer. Not even on the Congo collapse, with its humiliating horrors and its threat of bringing the cold war into the heart of Africa, could the new independent states act in unison. And what hard choices are presented to them! Dr. Nkrumah [1] entered into helpful economic relations with Israel—a country so well qualified to offer assistance to Africa—but he found at the Casablanca Conference that he had to join with Egypt in condemning his friend as a neo-colonialist tool of the West. How embarrassing at the African conference table to have to confront Ethiopia and Somalia with their envenomed frontier dispute! How hard, too, for new rulers, who dreamed perhaps of Pan-Africa, or even of West African federation, to abandon the shining new power and honour of complete sovereign independence! It is surely the obligation as well as the interest of the Western powers, and especially of their former rulers, to help these new nations overcome their differences and co-operate and where possible federate into larger units that will give Africa strength at home and abroad.

The new states take over, of course, the legacy of division left by the colonial powers. West Africa, especially, was shared out by France and Britain in a most haphazard way. The powers differed in so much more than language. How strange to see the cultural differences between the two nations mirrored on the broken surface of Africa! France consciously took up the torch of Rome. Her faith was in universal human reason and in unity through government, law, and culture, and she tried to hold all her colonies within the embrace of a greater France. But African nationalism was strong enough to demand her sudden and complete surrender to the same independence and fragmentation that were the end product of Britain's very different policy. But for France and for her colonies the past may prove to be not all lost. Again like Rome, France called her provincials to the councils in her capital, and many of the new African leaders learned high-level politics in equal association with Frenchmen in Paris, an advantage that no leaders in ex-British Africa can match.

But in the former British colonies there are many more Africans than in the ex-French colonies who have had experience in handling local affairs at different levels, from the quasi-parliaments of legislative councils down to tribal chieftainship and councils. France, with her ideas of centralization and her belief in equality, had little respect for

[1] Kwame Nkrumah (1909–   ): Prime Minister of the Gold Coast (1952–57), which became the Republic of Ghana in 1957. Since 1960 President of Ghana and Commander in Chief of the Armed Forces. Educated in the United States and at London University, Dr. Nkrumah was the first non-white African premier to attend the Commonwealth Conference in 1957. [Editor's note.]

tribal hierarchy and custom. . . . . But, to give the other side, on the southern rim of the Sahara I met one of the veiled Tuareg with his camels, and tried to learn his opinion of French administration. "But, madame!" he said, drawing himself up to the height of his slender, wiry frame, "I am a French citizen."

This is France's old magic, her power to give herself to those who could reach up to accept the gift. Long ago, in mid-eighteenth century North America, [the British] agent with the Red Indians, Sir William Johnson, exclaimed in jealous admiration that only the French could prove that an Indian hunter could become a civilized member of society. This secret weapon of assimilation stands France in good stead today. Nearly all her West African states keep their social and economic links with her, and this even while she continues to fight her Algerian rebels, who presented too hard an Islamic surface for her assimilative influences to pierce. Most of her former Negro provinces, now small independent states, are bound by need to accept the generous help she gives them in staff and economic privileges, and her outstanding assistance in finance. But, even if all these ties should fray or break, even though Guinea and Mali have struck their independent attitudes, it seems certain that what was French Negro Africa will long retain the deep intelligible pattern of French influence. This is because, with all her mistakes, she gave the African élite what they valued more than anything else in the world, what [Britain] so long failed to give them, the respect of equality. . . . .

The Africans of the former French and British colonies look out on the ex-Belgian Congo, a sight bitter to African hope and pride, for it reveals not only Belgium's great miscalculation, but also what Africa can still be without adequate help from the outside world. Farther south the prospect is much easier for them to judge. South Africa and the Portuguese colonies exhibit the unyielding supremacy of white over black. While these situations exist they can be condemned utterly, and all colonialism, past and present, can, when occasion demands, be associated with their condemnation. And all Western policy will also be condemned for tolerating them, while Communist propaganda is given its maximum opportunity.

.   .   .   .

As Britain and France step back to the sidelines, the United States steps forward to join them there. This new presence—let us confess it— was not at first easy for Britain to accept. It seemed sometimes as if Americans were saying to the Africans, even while Britain was engaged in the final delicate transfer of power: "*We* understand the meaning of freedom. We wrested it ourselves from these same colonialists, and once we have cleared away the last relics of British control, we can get down to the real business of helping you."

If some individuals *did* give this impression, they did injustice to their nation as a whole. America, like other nations, includes brash young nationalists and hard-faced businessmen. But she has been ready to put her great wealth into the service of the world as no other nation has ever done. She has bred specialists, indeed statesmen, in philanthropy who have so committed themselves to this complex, world-wide business of international aid that they have almost forgotten any particular American interest. America's concern with Africa came late, but, characteristically, she has made a remarkably quick start. A very few years ago the evidences of American concern with Africa could have been listed in a brief pamphlet: today a fat volume would be needed. It would include the many activities of the government itself, its diplomacy, its complex machinery for aid and service, the great philanthropic trusts, the universities, the business world, the Christian missions, and many more facets of American life that are now turned towards Africa.

. . . .

Confronting America, and also reaching out to Africa, stand Russia and her satellite powers, joining in the struggle to win the minds of the non-Western world. The achievement of independence lays Africa's new states wide open not only to the influence, but now to the activities, of the Communist states. The colonial powers used their authority to put up barriers against this influence. The inevitable response of the awakening African nationalists was: "If *you* are so much against Communism, there clearly must be something in it for *us*." And they found something—the practical example of Russia's rapid advance in industry, agriculture, and education. They were struck, too, by the absolute racial equality that Russia preaches and is believed to practise in her vast empire, though there race is a minor problem.

The Communists have at least two potential holds over the young African states. One concerns the matter of economic aid, and with this I shall deal in a moment. The other is education. Africans' thirst for education is such that they would accept it from the devil himself. So an ever-increasing stream of students flows into Russia. There they first learn the language and then spend several years at colleges or universities. A Peoples' Friendship University, significantly renamed the Lumumba [2] University, has been established in Moscow. It offers long courses of training, ultimately to 4,000 students, many of whom will be Africans. To counter Russia's own ignorance, serious research work on African sociology and history is now being carried out at Moscow and Leningrad universities—and need I add that African history is being rewritten? Meanwhile, Russia and the satellite states direct upon Africans, and especially young Africans and trade unionists, a spreading complex of agencies.

What are their chances of success? So far it is estimated that of the world's 40,000,000 Communists only about 50,000 are in Africa, and these mostly in the extreme north and south. Communists, indeed, are somewhat baffled by their failure to find in Africa—at least outside South Africa—the necessary stage-setting within which to play out the implacable drama of their revolution. Where is the dispossessed, land-hungry peasantry? Too few, too localized. The urban proletariat? Too few, again; too embryonic. The bourgeoisie, ripe for liquidation? Too few in most regions; too essential in others. Some revolutions, yes—but mostly such peaceful revolutions! With many of the expected Marxist necessities absent, some very improper elements are strongly present: racialism, nationalism, tribalism, and, surely, not a little personality cult. Among pagan, Christian, and Moslem there is also a deep belief in another world which makes them allergic to any anti-God campaign. And remember that on a map of religions Islam can be shown coming down over the great shoulders of Africa like a cape. Perhaps the strongest obstacle to Communism is . . . the passion of Africans to escape from all subjection. They are therefore determined not to get rid of the domination of one set of white men only to fall under that of another.

The Communist theorists are troubled by all this, but not dismayed. They can wait. They believe that in time the developments which their theory demands will, indeed must, come about and then what they call scientific socialism will swallow up all these regrettable errors.

Does it seem strange to us that Africans should appear to be so open to influence from a state which has not allowed a single [one]

---

[2] Patrice Lumumba (1925–61): Congolese political leader and first premier of the Republic of the Congo from June to September, 1960. When independence was followed by murder, riot, rape, and the secession of Katanga province, Lumumba appealed to the United Nations for military assistance. Once the United Nations Emergency Force had arrived in the Congo, however, he began to vilify Secretary General Hammarskjold and to demand the withdrawal of all white United Nations troops. Unable to reunite Katanga to the Republic, Lumumba was ousted from office in September, placed under arrest, and later killed by tribesmen in the self-proclaimed republic of Katanga. [Editor's note.]

of its own many dependencies to escape its power, which has bloodily repressed any "nationalist" stirrings, deported whole peoples, and in some places planted new lands with Russian settlers? It should *not* seem strange. The Africans are still held in the emotions of their revolt against the power and influence of the West. It is from *that* standpoint that they look out upon the world. For them the light falls on Russia's challenge to the West; Russia's offers of help; her achievements; her purposeful energy. The darker sides both of theory and of practice still lie in the shadow.

China stands beside Russia here. She, too, is stepping up every sort of activity in Africa: offering education, including that in guerrilla warfare; sending experts and entertainers; and diffusing a growing volume of influence by radio. She has some advantages over Russia. She suffered herself at the hands of the imperialists. And she has carried out an amazingly thorough communist revolution through her peasantry. Moreover, her people can be regarded as coloured—at least they are not white.

There is also the matter of economic aid. The subject is a jungle of facts and figures, of changing theories and difficult practices. I must skirt around it. One thing is clear. Africa is going to make an immense demand on the rest of the world. A dangerous discrepancy yawns between the hopes of Africans and their capacity to attain them. The Western nations increased their own wealth and their skills— the two are really indivisible—over many years during which governments, under capitalist influence, were able to impose under-consumption on the masses. The sudden wholesale enfranchisement of the poor and inexperienced masses in Africa makes that discipline impossible there—even if we wished to see it repeated. What then? The capital must be supplied from outside? But Africa no longer offers the security that enabled colonial governments to obtain a flow of capital. Will the Western powers therefore make adequate, steadily maintained financial sacrifices for political ends?

It is on this economic side that the Communist states have their greatest opportunity. They control all their own economic forces and can deploy them when and where they will. The new African leaders rule people of immense poverty and immense expectations. A population graph will show a mounting line while the agricultural price index, unless the Western powers can help to stabilize it, will zigzag dangerously. Popular disappointment, tribal disunity, and other difficulties may tempt African governments to increasingly dictatorial methods. If so, Communist tutors will be ready to show them their techniques of control. More likely, the Communists will direct against the old leaders the impatient young men as these return a few years hence from Marxist academies.

. . . .

We may hope that Africa will obtain donations of steel mills from Russia and will learn rice-growing from the Chinese without having to pay the full political price: that the difficulty of helping Africa may teach moderation even to Communists, or that inter-Communist rifts may weaken their offensive. But we cannot sit back and *hope* that this will happen and that Africa will retain our gradualist and liberal traditions, or return to them. The struggle being waged in Europe and Asia and South America is only now being extended to this fourth continent. Disunity, poverty, and inexperience make Negro Africa a vulnerable region. And in South Africa it exposes a tempting Achilles' heel.

On our side, we shall not find the African states easy to help. They ask, indeed demand, financial aid from their rich but hesitant suitors while they remain determined in no way to compromise their political chastity in return. The aid they accept must not even bear the moral taint of philanthropy.

It may be that . . . I have erred on the side of pessimism. Not that I would take back any of the fears I have voiced. But perhaps we should allow a little more for that incalculable factor, human nature. Africa, or parts of it, may yet surprise us. African human nature is undergoing a crisis. It is not enough for Africa's peoples, as it is not enough for any peoples dominated by the West, to escape from Western political power. The crushed mind and the wounded dignity have to recover. As we have seen in Asia, there are three possible reactions. One, generally the first, is for subjected peoples to try to reach out with both hands to appropriate the new Western model. This early reaction has often bred a small generation of those who have thus been assimilated. When the Western presence withdraws and the forces of nationalism advance, this generation may find itself stranded and lonely between the two forces. A second reaction is to reject the West, to endeavour to revive and assert the native culture, and especially, where possible, its religion. The third possibility is to attempt a synthesis of the two, not only—as is almost unavoidable—at the more superficial level, but at the deepest level of religion and philosophy, a task of the greatest difficulty and value. . . .

SELECT BIBLIOGRAPHY

THE OLD EMPIRE OF SPAIN

Carney, James J. "Early Spanish Imperialism," *Hispanic American Historical Review*, XIX (1939), 138–46.

Cunningham, Charles H. "The Institutional Background of Spanish American History," *Hispanic American Historical Review*, I (1918), 24–39.

Davies, Reginald T. *The Golden Century of Spain, 1501–1621*. London: 1937.

v. d. Kroef, J. M. "Francisco de Vitoria and the Nature of Colonial Policy," *The Catholic Historical Review*, XXXV, No. 2 (July, 1949), 129–62.

Merriman, R. B. *Rise of the Spanish Empire in the Old World and in the New*. 4 vols. New York: 1918–34.

Parry, J. H. *The Spanish Theory of Empire in the 16th Century*. Cambridge, Eng.: 1940.

Simpson, L. B. *The Encomienda in New Spain: Forced Native Labor in the Spanish Colonies, 1492–1550*. 2nd ed.; Berkeley, Calif.: 1950.

THE OLD EMPIRE OF PORTUGAL

Boxer, Charles R. *The Dutch in Brazil, 1624–1654*. Oxford: 1957.

Figueiredo, Fidelino. "The Geographical Discoveries and Conquests of the Portuguese," *Hispanic American Historical Review*, VI (February–August, 1926), 47–70.

———. *Four Centuries of Portuguese Expansion, 1415–1825*. Johannesburg: 1961.

———. *The Golden Age of Brazil, 1695–1750*. Berkeley: 1962.

———. *Race Relations in the Portuguese Colonial Empire, 1415–1825*. London: 1963.

Greenlee, William B. "The First Half Century of Brazilian History," *Mid-America*, 25, No. 2 (April, 1943), 91–120.

Haring, Clarence H. *Empire in Brazil*. Cambridge, Mass.: 1958.

Lima, M. Oliveira. *The Evolution of Brazil Compared with that of Spanish and Anglo-Saxon America*. Stanford, Calif.: 1914.

Marchant, A. *From Barter to Slavery*. Baltimore: 1942.

Martin, Percy A. "Portugal in America," *Hispanic American Historical Review*, XVII (1937), 182–210.

Morison, S. E. *Portuguese Voyages to America in the Fifteenth Century*. Cambridge, Eng.: 1940.

THE BRITISH EMPIRE, OLD AND NEW

Bennett, G., ed. *The Concept of Empire* . . . *1774–1947*. London: 1953, 1962.

Bodelsen, C. A. *Studies in Mid-Victorian Imperialism*. Reprint; London: 1960.

Burt, A. L. *The Evolution of the British Empire and Commonwealth from the American Revolution*. Boston: 1956.

Gipson, L. H. *The British Empire before the American Revolution*. 8 vols. Vols. I–III revised; New York: 1958–60.

Guttridge, G. H. *The Colonial Policy of William III in America and the West Indies*. Cambridge, Eng.: 1922.

Harlow, Vincent T. *The Founding of the Second British Empire, 1763–1793*. London: 1952.

Knaplund, Paul. *The British Empire, 1815–1939*. New York: 1941.

Mellor, George R. *British Imperial Trusteeship, 1783–1850*. London: 1951.

Newton, A. P. *A Hundred Years of British Empire*. London: 1940.

Schuyler, R. L. *The Fall of the Old Colonial System*. New York: 1945.

Semmel, Bernard. *Imperialism and Social Reform*. London: 1960.

Stokes, Eric. *The English Utilitarians and India*. New York: 1959.

Thornton, A. P. *The Imperial Idea and Its Enemies*. London: 1959.

Walker, Eric A. *The British Empire. Its Structure and Spirit, 1497–1953*. London: 1953.

Williamson, J. A. *A Short History of British Expansion*. New York: 1954.

Winks, Robin W., ed. *British Imperialism: Gold, God, Glory*. New York: 1963.

THE FRENCH EMPIRE, OLD AND NEW

Betts, Raymond F. *Assimilation and Association in French Colonial Theory, 1890–1914*. New York: 1961.

Cole, Charles W. *Colbert and a Century of French Mercantilism*. 2 vols. New York: 1939.

Deschamps, Hubert. *The French Union*. Paris: 1956.

Murphy, Agnes. *The Ideology of French Imperialism, 1871–1881*. Washington: 1948.

Priestley,. Herbert I. *France Overseas: A Study of Modern Imperialism*. New York: 1938.

———. *France Overseas through the Old Regime: A Study of European Expansion*. New York: 1939.

Roberts, Stephen H. *History of French Colonial Policy, 1870–1925*. 2 vols. London: 1929, Edinburgh: 1963.

THE GERMAN COLONIAL EMPIRE

Aydelotte, William O. *Bismarck and British Colonial Policy. The Problem of South West Africa, 1883–1885*. Philadelphia: 1937.

Brunschwig, Henri. *L'Expansion allemande outre-mer du XVe siècle à nos jours*. Paris: 1957.

Rudin, Harry R. *Germans in the Cameroons, 1884–1914.* New Haven, Conn.: 1938.

Taylor, A. J. P. *Germany's First Bid for Colonies, 1884–1885.* London: 1938.

Townsend, Mary E. *Origins of Modern German Colonialism, 1871–1885.* New York: 1921.

———. *The Rise and Fall of Germany's Colonial Empire, 1884–1918.* New York: 1930.

COLONIAL RULE AND COLONIAL INDEPENDENCE

Carrington, C. E. *The Liquidation of the British Empire.* London: 1961.

Cobban, Alfred. *National Self-Determination.* New York: 1945.

Curtin, Philip D. *Two Jamaicas: The Role of Ideas in a Tropical Colony, 1830–1865.* Cambridge, Mass.: 1955.

Emerson, Rupert. *Malaysia: A Study in Direct and Indirect Rule.* New York: 1937.

———. *From Empire to Nation: The Rise to Self-Assertion of Asian and African Peoples.* Cambridge, Mass.: 1960.

Evans, E. W. *The British Yoke.* London: 1949.

Hancock, W. K. *The Wealth of Colonies.* Cambridge, Eng.: 1950.

Rose, Saul, ed. *Politics in Southern Asia.* London: 1963.

Strachey, John. *The End of Empire.* New York: 1960.

Ward, John W. *British Policy in the South Pacific, 1786–1893.* Sydney: 1950.

Woodruff, Philip [pseud.], *The Men Who Ruled India,* 2 vols. (London, New York: 1954.)

Wright, Martin. *The Development of the Legislative Council, 1606–1945.* London: 1946.

AFRICA

Apter, David E. *The Gold Coast in Transition.* Princeton, N.J.: 1955.

Coleman, James S. *Nigeria: Background to Nationalism.* Berkeley, Calif.: 1958.

Curtin, Philip. *African History.* New York: 1963.

———. *The Image of Africa: British Ideas and Action, 1780–1850.* Madison, Wis.: 1964.

Davidson, Basil. *The African Awakening.* London: 1955.

Deschamps, H. *L'Eveil Politique Africain.* Paris: 1952.

Duffy, James. *Portuguese Africa.* Cambridge, Mass.: 1959.

Haines, Grove, ed. *Africa Today.* Baltimore: 1955.

Hodgkin, Thomas. *Nationalism in Colonial Africa.* London: 1958.

———. *African Political Parties.* Harmondsworth, Eng.: 1961.

Lüthy, H. "The Passing of the European Order," *Encounter*, IX, No. 5 (November, 1957).

Macmillan, William M. *Bantu, Boer, and Briton: The Making of the South African Native Problem*. London: 1929.

———. *Africa Emergent*. London: 1958.

———. *The Road to Self Rule: A Study in Colonial Evolution*. London: 1959.

Oliver, Roland. *Sir Harry Johnston and the Scramble for Africa*. London: 1957.

———. *The Missionary Factor in East Africa*. London: 1952.

——— and Fage, J. D. *A Short History of Africa*. New York: 1963.

Perham, Margery. *Native Administration in Nigeria*. London: 1962.

——— ed. *Colonial and Comparative Studies*. London: 1948.

Stillman, (... orld*. Chicago: 1955.

GENERAL

Clark, Grover. *A Place in the Sun*. New York: 1936.

———. *The Balance Sheets of Imperialism* . . . New York: 1936.

Hallgarten, George W. F. *Imperialismus vor 1914*. 2 Vols., Munich: 1951, 2d ed., I, 1963.

Koebner, R. *Empire*. Cambridge, Eng.: 1961.

——— and Schmidt, H. D. *Imperialism: The Story and Significance of a Political Word, 1840–1960*. Cambridge, Eng.: 1963.

Moon, Parker T. *Imperialism and World Politics*. New York: 1926.

Niebuhr, R. *The Structure of Nations and Empires*. New York: 1959.

Townsend, M. E. and Peake, C. H. *European Colonial Expansion since 1871*. Philadelphia: 1941.

Winslow, E. M. *The Pattern of Imperialism: A Study in the Theories of Power*. New York: 1948.

Woolf, Leonard. *Economic Imperialism*. London: 1921.